Na'auao Ola Hawaii

Hawaiian Principles and Practices of Being Well

Maka'ala Yates

BALBOA
PRESS

A DIVISION OF HAY HOUSE

Balboa Press books may be ordered through booksellers or by contacting:

Balboa Press
A Division of Hay House
1663 Liberty Drive
Bloomington, IN 47403
www.balboapress.com
1 (877) 407-4847

Because of the dynamic nature of the Internet, any web addresses or links contained in this book may have changed since publication and may no longer be valid. The views expressed in this work are solely those of the author and do not necessarily reflect the views of the publisher, and the publisher hereby disclaims any responsibility for them.

Nothing in this book is intended to provide treatment for any disease, disability, or medical condition, or to substitute for personal, individual medical care from a qualified physician. The reader is advised to check with his or her own physician prior to following any recommendations given in this book or any of its references. Every attempt has been made to provide accurate information, however, the reader is on notice that the information in this book has been compiled and written to address general principles. It is not intended as specific advice for any individual. Thus, the personal application of any information provided herein is the sole responsibility of the user and, if implemented, would be applied at his/her own risk.

Any people depicted in stock imagery provided by Thinkstock are models, and such images are being used for illustrative purposes only. Certain stock imagery © Thinkstock.

Printed in the United States of America.

ISBN: 978-1-4525-1923-4 (sc)
ISBN: 978-1-4525-1924-1 (e)

Balboa Press rev. date: 08/01/2014

This book is dedicated to my mother,
Marion "Dolly" Yates.

Her beacon of love, compassion and *ho'okupu* (her gift
of giving unconditionally) still shines and inspires me to
carry on this light long after she left to go home.

Epigraph

Ua mau ke ea o ka ʻaina i ka pono

The life, breath, and spirit of the land, will always remain in the right relationship with the people and all living things.

Contents

E pule kakou na mua ka heluhelu i keia puke

E ke Kumukahi mau loa, ke kunou makou mamua i kou alo me ka ha'aha'a. Nana ia makou me ka lokomaika'i. Mahalo aku nei ia 'oe e ke kumukahi no na mea apau. Nou i ha'awi mai ia na po'e kanaka, 'oia ho'i, ka la, ka ua, ka honua, ka moana, na hoku, na mea 'aka'aka, na mea kaumaha, ame ko makou mau mea i a'o ai.

'Alaka'i mai 'oe ia makou i na la apau nolaila, hiki ia makou ke ho'omaopopo ia ai na mea pono o ke ao. E ha'i mai 'oe i kou mau kapu pau'ole, a e launa aloha mai kou 'uhane me makou i keia manawa, a i ka manawa pau'ole. Aloha e.

My prayer to you before reading this book

In the spirit of love, peace, harmony, and respect to the One Source that is omnipresent, which exists in all things, let us humbly embrace all truths, all people, and all possibilities. Thank you Divine Spirit for all things that are provided to us. Continue to look upon us with kindness and generosity. Thank you for the sun, the rain, our planet, the ocean, the stars, laughter, sadness, and our unique individual gifts.

Guide us each and everyday so that we may better understand our true purpose in life. Let us all reconnect our sacredness and endless love from our soul to the One Source and to all people now and forever. Love always.

Maka'ala

Foreword

This book from Dr. Maka'ala is based on a delicate and yet powerful blend of time-tested traditional knowledge and scientific wisdom. The teachings are well researched and supported. The advice is extremely grounded and useful. At last we have a reliable resource on health and healing that combines the practical and the esoteric.

I have been looking forward to Maka'ala's first book for many years. For over a decade I've enjoyed his classes, Hawaiian sweat lodges (*Hale Pulo'u'lo'u*), stories, chants and songs at workshops in British Columbia, and on Kaua'i, Maui and the Big Island. You hold in your hands a unique and valuable compilation of decades of his teachings in traditional Hawaiian knowledge combined with research and proven wisdom.

Beginning with his genealogy chant, as Polynesian tradition dictates, we get a chance to explore valuable esoteric thoughts. Who are you? How do you define yourself? Is it by your looks, job, possessions, relationships or skills? Is it by something more timeless, encompassing your deep essence and true nature? Awareness of your ancestry (or *whakapapa* as it is called here in *Aotearoa*) is a way to honor and comprehend the connections we all have to one another, not only in the present moment, but also into both the past (our ancestors) and the future (our children and grandchildren). In a traditional Hawaiian perspective, each of us is deeply connected to the past and future, and this realization further extends into our relationship with the Earth, which sustains us all, and the very stardust from which we were born. This esoteric knowledge is no secret, yet it is so deeply profound that few can fathom it much less identify with it.

Maka'ala can and does understand this and has for many decades. Additionally, he helped create awareness of it while participating in the original 1976 Hokulea Voyage of Discovery between Tahiti and the

Hawaiian Islands that launched the 'Hawaiian Renaissance', and has since taken full responsibility for his role in it. Furthermore, he chose to become a *kumu* (teacher) and *kauka* (doctor) for the people, teaching us and caring for the perpetuation of cultural truth, wellness and health. He does this out of a sincere, steadfast and deeply committed connection and reverence for his own *whakapapa* and teachers. This is also true of his understanding of both Hawaiian and Western principles of holistic health, diet and lifestyle.

Terms like traditional ancient Kahuna wisdom, Hawaiian secret knowledge and indigenous magic are often thrown around haphazardly and can be misleading. When it comes to marketing various Hawaiian teachings, courses and information to the general public, much is promoted without sacredness or authenticity. The mystique and popularity of indigenous wisdom has become a 'wow' factor for increasing sales. The logic implied is that since Hawai'i is rich with strong *mana*, timeless attraction, magnificent beauty and fascinating culture, anything from Hawai'i must carry the same mystique.

Maka'ala provides us with information based on natural law that we can count on. When we look deeply into the universal, natural ways of maintaining health and vitality, we can find reliable principles and even predictable patterns of cause and effect that govern how our bodies maintain homeostasis or balance. This provides us with a platform for wellness of body, mind and spirit. Lack of balance leaves us less than whole and vulnerable to disease. Even if we study nutrition, physiology, genetics, etc., we can easily become entangled in a maze of different opinions and opposing directions for healthful choices. This is especially true when we try to navigate through corporate-driven propaganda meant to persuade us to compromise our beliefs and buying habits. It can be very daunting, to say the least, however, we can learn to be well with diligent discernment. We can re-discover and utilize natural laws and indigenous wisdom to successfully find our way back to true wellness, health and balance.

Natural laws, like the law of gravity on our planet, are non negotiable. I have found that Maka'ala's teachings have always been committed to natural laws and principles. He has wholeheartedly explored the absolute truth of these laws and shared them with his students and patients in order to assist each one in their own healing and self-responsibility.

So enjoy and read onward with an open mind, teachable spirit and humble heart. Apply the principles suggested herein and you will begin the voyage of discovery and open the door to greater wellness.

Aloha pumehana,
Nancy S Kahalewai
www.HowToLomilomi.com
23 June 2014
New Zealand

Polynesian Protocol

Traditionally, from a Hawaiian and from a Polynesian perspective, it is always proper protocol to share a person's individual chant of who they are, where they're from and what family lineage they belong to when first meeting other Polynesian "cousins." The two forms of this traditional protocol are called, *ku'auhau,* a lineage chant, and *kuamo'o,* a life pathway chant. *Ku'auhau* is what I have often heard used growing up in Kona on the Big Island of Hawaii. When it pertained to the genetic or family heritage, the term *'ohana ku'auhau* was used. This involved lineages from both sides of a person's parents that typically covered at least eight generations back. When describing your lineage of teachers, it was called *kumu a'o ku'auhau.*

The life pathway chant was sometimes called *kaona kuamo'o,* which meant that there was a hidden meaning within the chant that was describing who you are and what you are here to do while in physical form and can include metaphors. This chant is usually created and recited after a child is born and is done by a village elder, *kupuna,* who paid strict attention as the soul entered into physical form and finally into the physical world. It was not uncommon for this type of *kaona kuamo'o* to be created or adjusted sometime after a child is born due to the late unfolding of their specific characteristics. One of my Hawaiian teachers, auntie Margaret Machado, received her *kaona kuamo'o* from her grandfather at the age of eight. Her chant lasted many hours, which began with the use of the ceremonial *ha.* This is when the elder's breath is used on different parts of the body before the chant was recited for the first time. A *kaona kuamo'o* can be a poetic chant describing the specific spiritual aspects of that particular soul and is typically expressed in specific ceremonies and events.

When I was born in 1948, I was never given a *kaona kuamo'o* nor did others that I knew from my village. As far as I know, with the exception of auntie Margaret, none were performed since the days of my great grandfather and grandmother from my village in Kona, Hawai'i.

I never gave my genealogy much thought until I first visited Tahiti on Hokule'a in 1976. This was a historic voyage on a traditional Hawaiian double hull canoe that sailed from Hawaii to Tahiti and back with no modern navigational instruments. A documentary film of this voyage was produced by the National Geographic Society, which was called, "*Hokule'a*." While traveling throughout Tahiti, I noticed that the average Tahitian could recite their *ku'auhau* at least eight generations from both sides of their parents. This intrigued me and inspired me to learn more about my own lineage chant, which lead me to understand the different forms of traditional genealogical chants.

It took me many years of deep meditation and purpose to finally come up with my own *kaona kuamo'o* that best describes my soul and what I am here to do while in this dimensional construct. It was also important for me to create my own lineage chant of Hawaiian teachers, *kumu a'o ku'auhau*, before I could pursue any traditional ventures like teaching *Mana Lomi*[1] or *Ho'oponopono*[2] at the next level. Without this I wouldn't feel complete as a person and I wouldn't feel as connected to my ancestors who have crossed over into the Spirit world. I couldn't start writing this book for example, until this was completed, because my words and who or what I represent could appear disconnected. Another Polynesian reading this book may not feel a connection with my words and therefore my ancestors. This is true for anyone else reading this book for that matter. The difference in outcome is a book filled with a soul versus a book filled with words.

---

[1] Mana Lomi® is a form of *lomilomi*, which is a traditional bodywork therapy handed down through the generations, that focuses on problem solving physical maladies. See supplemental pages at the end of this book for more information.

[2] Ho'opono or ho'oponopono is a Hawaiian philosophy and practice of living in balance each and everyday of our lives. See chapter 1.

For the purpose of this book, I will share both my *kaona kuamo'o* and my *kumu a'o ku'auhau*. I have provided the English translation as accurately as possible for those that do not speak Hawaiian.

Thank you for taking the time to read this book.

Mahalo nui loa
Maka'ala

He 'Oli No Na Kupuna 'o Maka'ala
(He Kaona Kuamo'o)

He one hanau 'o Honaunau
He 'aina kapu kahiku
He pilina Ka'awaloa
He kūhohonu i ka papaku o ka
moana
No laila mai ka na'auao

Pau 'akoakoa ka na'auao
'O ka ho'ala ia
E ala, e ala a'e, e ala mai e
'O ka lamaku ma'ama'ama
'O ka pilina, ua pa'a

He makani Pilihala ko Ka'awaloa
He kilohana kapa no ke keiki
hanau
He leo aloha pa'e mai
Ku ana Mo'olau me Kamailolo
Na Kipapa Nui

'O Kipapa Nui ka mua
I pae mai ma ka 'aina
Nana ka hokeo
I ola ai ka po
I ala a'e ka maka powehi

Na Kipapa Nui
'O Maka'ala
I kahu hokeo malamalama
E kupa'a, e 'onipa'a
A ala mai ka ikaika o loko

He 'olu Honaunau
He pilina na'auao
No lalo o ke kai
E ku kia'i mau ana
Me ka mana'olana, aloha e

Chant for the Ancestors of Maka'ala

Honaunau is his birthplace
A land that has long been sacred
Ka'awaloa is its distant sister
A land far beneath the sea
Where the wisdom keepers reside

The wisdom keepers have gathered
It is the awakening
Arise!
Arise keeper of the torch
The bonds remain intact

The Pilihala wind of Ka'awaloa
Is like a precious blanket for the
newborn
Carrying the voices
Mo'olau and Kamailolo
Of Kipapa Nui

Kipapa Nui was the first to come
From the land far beneath the sea
His famous bowl of light
Filled the darkness with divine life
To awaken the ones that couldn't see

From the line of Kipapa Nui
Comes the life of Maka'ala
To carry forward the bowl of light
With enduring hope &
commitment
So others realize their true power

Refreshing is the land of Honaunau
The connection to the wise elders
Residing in a land beneath the sea
Ever so watchful and mindful
With the hope and love for all

He 'Oli No Na Kumu A'o 'O Maka'ala

Na Makua Kane John Peal Yates na mo'olelo
No ka mana ho'ola o na kupuna e pa'a hou ai ka iwi
No ka hale ho'ola
No ke ahupua'a, no ke kuleana kanaka
A me ke kai ho'oma'ema'e kino, ho'omaha na'au, ho'olana 'uhane

Na Kupuna Phoebe ka lomi i a'o mai i ke ono o na makahiki
'O ka 'ike o na kupuna kai ho'oili 'ia mai
E ala mai ana ka ikaika lima ho'ola
E pua mai ana ka na'auao koli'u o ka wa kahiko
E 'upu a'e ana ho'i ka hali'a

Na Kupuna Margaret ka ho'ala
Puoho ka moe, he moe uhane
Ua ala ka maka, ua 'ikea ke kuleana o keia wa no
'O ka lomilomi me ka la'au, 'o ia ke kahua
O ka ho'ola Hawai'i ku'una

Na Kupuna Edith ka 'olelo me ka mo'omeheu i a'o mai
'O ka ho'ola o ka lua
'O ka pana o ka 'olelo
'O na mele a kahiko, 'o naä mele hou
'O na mo'olelo o ka wa i hala e pono ai ka noho 'ana

Na Kupuna Mona ka ho'oponopono
Nana i kuhikuhi mai i na loina me na hana ku'una
Ke koho 'ana i ke keiki nana ka 'ike e malama ho'omau
E mau mai ai ka 'ike a me ka na'auao kahiko
I pili ka 'ohana, mai na kupuna a na mo'opuna

'O 'A'ala ka 'opio piha na'auao
Ua akaka ka mana'o no ke 'ano o ka Hawai'i
No ke ahuapua'a, no ka 'olelo, no ka hana ku'una
Ua a'o mai i ka mo'aukala Hawai'i
A me na loli i nawaliwali ai ka mo'omeheu

Na Kupuna 'Iolani ka hula me ke oli
Me ka pilina o ke kanaka me na mea pau o ka honua
Ka 'oe a ke kai, 'o kana 'olelo ia
Ka 'oni a ka la'au, ka holo a ka holoholona, 'o ka lakou 'olelo ia
No loko mai o ka na'au ka 'olelo 'oia'i'o a ke kanaka

Na Kupuna Mornah ke akaka o ka ka 'onaeao
He pilina 'uhane ko na mea a pau
'O ka ho'oponopono ke ki'ina pono
'O ke kilo i na 'ouli o ke ao
'O na mele oli, na mo'oku'auhau kanaka

Na Kupuna Hale ka ho'opili, a pili ke kanaka me ka honua
He mea nui ka 'olelo me ka leo ma ka ho'ola
He koho ke kokua kaiaulu no kela la, keia la
Aia ke ola i keia manawa 'ano, 'o ka wa i hala, ua hala ia
E Mahalo i ka mea loa'a, e hau'oli i ka noho 'ana 'oiai he pokole wale
no ke ola

Chant For The Teachers of Maka'ala

From my dad, John Peal Yates, came the stories
Of the healing abilities from the old ones
From mending broken bones to the house of purification
To the ahupua'a and our living responsibilities
To the ocean for cleansing the body, mind and soul

From Kupuna Phoebe begins the lomi at six years old
The knowledge of the old ones passes through the bones
The connection of the touch begins to awaken
The energy and wisdom of the old ones start to surface
And feelings from within spark a remembrance

Kupuna Margaret starts the waking process
I suddenly realized the dream I was in
The past is severed and the present is embraced
It is the lomi and herbs that build the foundation
To the many forms of Hawaiian healing

Kupuna Edith taught the language and culture
The ancient lua is explained for healing
The rhythm of the language is shown
The old songs sang and new ones written
The stories of the past bring meaning to my life

Kupuna Mona teaches and lives ho'oponopono
The traditional ways are often shared
How the child was selected to carry on the work
To perpetuate and preserve ancient skills and knowledge
For family unity, it's the connection between children and grandparents

A'ala was a young spirit full of wisdom
Clear was her thoughts on the Hawaiian ways
From ahupua'a to language and traditions
She taught the history of the Hawaiian people
And the evolutionary changes of a diluted culture

Kupuna Iolani was a master especially in the Hula and chants
Her teachings were the connection to all things
The ocean speaking through its waves
The plants and animals speaking through their movements and tones
Always speak and feel from the heart to see your truth

Kupuna Morrnah brought clarity of the universe
The spiritual relationships to all things
The importance of ho'oponopono to bring balance
Understanding how to interpret and read the signs
From the chants to the stories of the origin of man

Kupuna Hale kept me grounded to Mother Earth
The language and its tones was important for healing
Giving back to the community a daily choice
Live in the moment and not the past
Appreciate all things and be joyous in this short life

Acknowledgements

My thanks (*mahalo*) and gratitude (*ho'omaika'i*) to:

- *Kumukahi* (One Source), which is omnipresent and fills the interspaces of all things within the universe. A Source that exists in all things and all life and intelligence comes from it.
- The many Hawaiian and non-Hawaiian medicine practitioners (*na kahuna la'au lapa'au*) that came before me, whose genius and courage enabled the development of the ideas and techniques presented in this book.
- My mother, Marion (Dolly) Correa for her unending encouragement for me to pursue my dreams.
- My life partner, best friend and wife, Renee Duval for her tireless support, and all her help getting this book completed.
- The long list of students who brought out the best in me in the thousands of workshops that I taught all over the globe.
- The persistence of friends, family members and students asking, "When will the book be done?"
- Cat DeBoni for her valuable editing feedback and review of this book.
- My *na kupuna* (elders) and na kumu (teachers) who are my lifetime mentors.

Mahalo nui loa

Hawaiian Pronunciation

The Hawaiian language has gone through incredible evolutionary changes over the last 200 years. From an ancient character written language (pre-warrior period) to an oral language (warrior period) to a written language again (missionary period). It is interesting to note that the very first Hawaiian language newspaper, and in fact the only newspaper west of the Rocky Mountains in the 1800s, was called *Ka Lama Hawaii* (the Hawaiian Luminary).

When the American missionaries arrived in 1820, they formulated a written Hawaiian language that attempted to change the tones and rhythm of our linguistic heritage, intentionally or not. Fortunately, the Hawaiians from the island of Ni'ihau (a privately owned island by the Robinson family near the island of Kauai) maintained the original language and its tones from the past. More importantly, it was on this tiny island that we found the ancient character written language hidden from the world for generations.

There are thirteen letters in the Hawaiian alphabet: five vowels (a, e, i, o, u) and eight consonants (h, k, l, m, n, p, w) including the *'okina* (') or glottal stop. An *'okina* makes a pause between syllables. It is a vocal break similar to the sound made from the phrase "oh – oh." My name for example, is spelled "Maka'ala." Where the 'okinia is located, you would have the sound like "ka – ah." Putting it all together, it would be pronounced Mahkah, pause, ahla. Not putting a pause in the word that has an *'okina* in it changes the meaning of that word. Maka'ala would go from "alert, awake, awareness," to makaala, which could mean, "eye road" or "next to the road." The kahakô or macron (straight line over the vowel) indicates an elongated vowel. To make a word plural, just add "na" before it. It's not correct to add an "s" after a Hawaiian word to make it plural. Notice that every word ends in a vowel similar to Italian.

Vowels: a e i o u
a is pronounced "ah" - like the "a" in about
e is pronounced "eh" - like the "a" in say
i is pronounced "ee" - like the first "i" in illicit
o is pronounced "oh" - like the "o" in go
u is pronounced "oo" – like the "oo" in hoot

Consonants: h k l m n p w'
All consonants are pronounced like their English counterparts with the exception of w. It is pronounced as a "v" when it follows the "i", and "e" letters. It is pronounced as a "w" when it follows "u" and "o" letters. When it starts a word or after "a" the "w" or "v" sound is acceptable. The name "Hawaii" is typically pronounced "hahvai – ee.

For the purpose of this book, some Hawaiian words have diacritical marks and others do not due to the ease and speed to get this book published in as many languages as possible. It would take a special word program to make correct diacritical marks, but it is hoped that the English translation will be sufficient for the reader to understand.

This brief introduction to the Hawaiian language pronunciation is included to give each reader a better feel for the tones and rhythm of a language that dates back to the origin of a Polynesian race.

Introduction

Before the *ipu kea* (white people) arrived in Hawaii in 1776, it was a known fact that the *kanaka maoli* (original Hawaiians) were very healthy and very strong. Their teeth were in perfect condition with no decay or misalignment and their average height was about 7 foot tall as evident from many of the bones excavated on the Big Island of Hawaii by my father and other Hawaiian road builders.

Not only were the original *kanaka maoli* healthy, but they also lived in harmony with each other on a set of islands not very large, and with only canoes to get them from island to island. In fact, in the 1700's on the peninsula in Ho'okena on the Big Island of Hawaii, there was an estimated population of thirty thousand people living in harmony with each other and the environment. They were practicing the Hawaiian principles of being well and they passed this information on to a few within the Hawaiian community who would listen. My training in this ancient wisdom of health started at the age of six and *lomilomi[3] was the entry point to the secrets of the ancients and their* treasure chest of healing.

According to the Office of Hawaiian Affairs (OHA), research and data in 2011 indicate "Native Hawaiians suffer some of the worst health inequities in the State of Hawai'i and rival disparate health conditions across the Continental U.S."

The following is a brief outline of some of the health problems as indicated by OHA (Papa Ola Lōkahi, N.D.; WHIAAPI Fact Sheet, N.D.).

- Native Hawaiians are over 5 times as likely to experience diabetes between the ages of 19-35 (11% vs. 2%) compared to non-Hawaiians.

---

[3] Lomi or lomilomi is a traditional form of bodywork therapy that works on the physical and energetics of that person. See supplemental pages.

- Native Hawaiians have the highest rate of deaths due to cancer compared to any other ethnic group in Hawai'i.
- Heart disease is a major cause of death and disability among Native Hawaiians. Native Hawaiians age 36-65 in Hawaii are nearly one and half times more likely to experience heart disease than other racial groups.
- Life expectancy amongst native Hawaiians is the lowest of all major ethnic groups in Hawai'i - 5 years less than the state average.
- They have the highest proportion of risk factors leading to illness & premature death: sedentary lifestyle, obesity, hypertension, smoking, acute drinking.
- Native Hawaiians are dying at younger ages than the general population—more than double the rate for the total population in those 25 years or younger.
- Cardiovascular disease accounts for 39% of native Hawaiian deaths.

According to the Asian and Pacific Islander American Health Forum, "Native Hawaiians have the highest rate of deaths due to cancer compared to any other ethnic group in Hawaii (229 per 100,000) and the third highest rate in the United States."

On one hand, we as Hawaiians are more susceptible to many so-called, "incurable diseases" known within the United States. On the other hand, the answer for perfect health is right in front of us as taught by and lived by our ancestors. What happened and why aren't we listening to the call of the ancient ones? Is the Hawaiian race destined to be the next extinct species? One thing is certain however, change is inevitable and the time for change is now!

The change I am speaking of is not limited to only Hawaiians. The health crisis throughout the world is rising at an alarming rate! According to the World Health Organization the following facts should be noted.

- One billion people lack access to health care systems.

- Non-communicable diseases, such as cardiovascular disease, cancer, diabetes and chronic lung diseases, cause 36 million deaths each year. This is almost two-thirds of the estimated 56 million deaths each year worldwide. (A quarter of these take place before the age of 60.)
- Cardiovascular diseases (CVDs) are the number one group of conditions causing death globally. An estimated 17.5 million people died from CVDs in 2005, representing 30% of all global deaths. Over 80% of CVD deaths occur in low- and middle-income countries.
- Over 7.5 million children under the age of 5 die from malnutrition and mostly preventable diseases, each year.
- In 2008, some 6.7 million people died of infectious diseases alone, far more than the number killed in the natural or man-made catastrophes that make headlines.

After many years working in the health care field, and my lifetime studies and practices as a Hawaiian medicine specialist, I have come to the conclusion that simple is better. I have integrated the old Hawaiian ways of living and its overall philosophies into modern life style practices. Na'auao Ola Hawaii is a book that is intended for all those who want a strong, healthy, functioning body. It is for those who want a practical guide & handbook, based on Hawaiian principles of being well, that work! It is my intention, as an instructor in the use of Hawaiian practices, to explain these concepts as simply as possible, so that readers of this book can realize their ideal health.

As the title suggests, this book deals with traditional Hawaiian principles that have worked for generations, especially during the pre-warrior period (400-1300 AD), and are not based on speculation. The deeper *aumakua* principle for example, deals with the idea that matter, mind, consciousness, and life are all manifestations of *Kumukahi* (One Source). For more information on *aumakua*, see supplemental pages at the back of this book. If you accept this idea as a possibility, you will find logical conclusions from this book that may change your life forever.

Today people from around the world are flocking to Hawaii to experience and learn "traditional" Hawaiian practices that only recently (last 30+ years) are starting to be revealed. These practices have been used successfully for thousands of years before the appearance of *ipukea* in Hawaii, and which are described in this book. The Hawaiian healing practice of *ho'oponopono* for example, is one of the most popular topics that people from around the world come to Hawaii to learn.

I can say that *Na'auao Ola Hawaii* works as evident by my years of clinical and teaching experiences. By changing our lifestyles and habits, we can prevent the tissues of our body from being destroyed beyond the tipping point from where it cannot recover.

If you want to be well and stay that way, it is important to take care of the inner workings of the body as well as give your whole mind to a *pono* way of thinking and living. The Hawaiian Practices and Principles of Being Well is a comprehensive and adequate guide to use for all your needs. If you focus on the way you think and take action (*ho'o*) as I will describe, and practice the principles diligently, you will get well. If you are already well, you will remain so.

Trusting that you will never give up until the realization of ideal health is yours, I give thanks (*mahalo*) to *na Kupuna* (the ancient ones) for their wisdom and knowledge.

Maka'ala Yates D.C.
Founder
Mana Lomi®
Indigenous Botanicals™

CHAPTER 1

Ho'oponopono
Living in Balance

To begin to understand the Hawaiian practices and principles of being well, we first must understand the basic concepts of *ho'oponopono,* sometimes referred to as *ho'opono.* It is a concept that is so vast and potentially complex that it commands a book to do it justice. However, as important as it is, I will attempt to provide a brief overview of this idea so that you can begin the process of letting go of those things that do not serve you anymore. Letting go of "dead weight" or negative emotional experiences and focusing on positive outcomes will be important steps in finding your balance to being well.

Ho'oponopono literally means "the action of being in balance/alignment." It is the act of living in harmony with all things, with all places and with all people. It applies to many levels of the human soul. In the Hawaiian language, when there is a double word like ponopono, it emphasizes the word being described. Ho'o is the action of that emphasized word.

Ho'oponopono was the primary concept that the ancient Hawaiians used to live in harmony with each other well before the first white man stepped on the islands of Hawaii. It is an idea that can help restore peace and prosperity to the world we live in. It is an understanding that we are all connected (*e piko kakou*) and that we are in this world to support and love each other. Every thought, action or words used affects everyone within one's community.

The basic foundation for all areas of pursuit such as healing the body, mind or soul is to live a conflict-free life. The goal is to clear the path or relationship of any imbalance created or unwanted burdens or accumulated problems. Learning to disconnect from negative energies or wrongful thinking is a simple and effective way of moving on with your life. It is a concept to allow your soul to expand. Holding on to negative emotional experiences can cause a contraction to the body leading to all kinds of negative outcomes. In my many years of clinical experience working with many health conditions, I have often seen immediate positive results when the patient severed the cord to deep traumatic energies.

I came across a short article in the Journal of the American Medical Association (JAMA, March 3, 1989 – vol 261, no. 9) with the title "Keola and the Kahuna." It was written by a Medical Doctor, a dermatologist from the Wilcox Hospital in Hawaii, on the island of Kauai. Paraphrasing the story, it described a 37-year-old man by the name of Keola who had a 1-year history of disabling hand and foot dermatitis. Part of his brief history was that his wife had had cancer and had her uterus removed about 1-year prior and could no longer conceive. She was okay with that but he wasn't. The MD noticed that the wife did most of the talking and Keola did most of the listening. After weeks of medical tests and treatments with no apparent results, the MD, out of frustration, suggested that Keola see a *Kahuna la'au lapa'au* (in this case a Hawaiian medicine master) on the Big Island of Hawaii whose name was Auntie Margaret Machado. A few weeks later Keola returned to the medical clinic and to the MD's astonishment he sees that Keola's rash was completely resolved. He asked Keola if he had seen the *Kahuna* on the Big Island and, surprisingly, the response was, "no". The article finishes by saying that "Patients like Keola are humbling. Western physicians are trained to diagnose disease and their proximate causes." The MD further speculated, "It was not the kahuna who healed here. Perhaps the bond of trust and caring that had grown among us was therapeutic."

I was still in Chiropractic school in Portland, Oregon when I read the article. I immediately contacted Auntie Margaret by telephone. She was someone that I had studied Hawaiian medicine with for about sixteen years. I asked her if she knew anything about this article, or Keola. She told me that Keola called her on the telephone and essentially gave her the same history as he did to the MD on Kauai. What the article didn't mention was that Keola was from the island of Ni'ihau and spoke mostly Hawaiian. This explains why his wife did all the talking. The first question Auntie Margaret asked Keola was, "Do you know *ho'oponopono?*" The Ni'ihau man quietly said, "yes." Auntie Margaret replied, "Then you know what to do!" The conversation between Auntie Margaret and Keola lasted about fifteen minutes yet in that brief moment he knew exactly what he had to do and more importantly, he knew he had all the tools to accomplish it. Within a few weeks Keola's skin cleared up. Through *ho'oponopono* he was able to get rid of the anger and disappointment he'd been harboring, which was contributing to his rash. He was able to accept his wife's inability to conceive, and he was ready to move on with his life. One final note about this article is that had the MD asked Keola if he had talked to Auntie Margaret, his answer would have been yes. The more specific we are in our questions the more specific the answers are, especially in the Hawaiian culture. The more specific your focus is on cutting the cord, the quicker the outcome is. Perhaps if the MD knew about the *ho'oponopono* prescription that the Big Island *Kahuna* gave to Keola, he might have titled the article "Keola and Ho'oponopono."

Ho'oponopono is the way to bring peace, harmony, love and wisdom into one's life and ultimately, the community, society, the world, and the universe.

Meditation is an important part of the practice of *ho'oponopono* because it can increase and refine the receptivity of the Divine consciousness (*Kumukahi*) within all things. Meditation is a way of reuniting the soul with our higher consciousness and with *Kumukahi*. The soul manifests its consciousness and *mana* (life-force) through the '*piko*' or centers of organic light within the human cerebrospinal axis. It is within this bodily prism that the soul consciousness and *mana* become identified with physical limitations.

Our body is programmable by language, tones, words or thoughts, all of which carry a frequency. The kind of frequency created is directly related to the desired outcome. Each individual must work on his or her inner processes, and personal development in order to establish a conscious communication with his/her DNA, which is our super-conductor that can store light, and therefore, information.

When a large group of people gets together with higher intentions, such as meditating on peace, violent potentials will dissolve. It is through meditation that all questions, all troubles, and all difficulties can eventually be resolved or answered.

The following is a sample of a simple Hawaiian meditation technique called "Alo Ha." The practice of meditation will be further explored in Chapter 14 (Ho'okuano'o).

Aloha

Alo refers to the connection we have to all things including source or *Kumukahi.*

Ha refers to the essence of life from where the evolutionary process unfolds. It is commonly used to describe the variations of breath.

Be aware of the inhale breath, and the exhale breath. Without forcing the process of breathing observe the inhale breath and visualize the '*Alo.*' Observe the exhale part of the breath and visualize the '*Ha.*'

This is beneficial while sitting, walking, running, exercising, standing in line at the grocery store or any of your favorite activities. This meditation technique is important to use when the mind wanders especially during meditation exercises or when having difficulty sleeping. Pay particular attention to your intentions during the inhale part of your breathing at all times before you exhale your words to others.

The objectives of *Ho'oponopono*:

- To release and severe (*'oki*) unwanted energetic cord(s) or connection with a person, place or thing.
- To restore balance (*kaulike*), harmony (*lokahi*), and tranquility (*maluhia*) within the self and outside the self.
- To manifest healing for yourself and others.
- Transform your consciousness by including qualities of conscious living such as:
  o Love, Kindness, Unity, Discernment, Patience, Responsibility, Humility, Grace, Mindfulness, Gratitude, Engaged Detachment, Compassion, Truthfulness, and Unconditional Giving.

For many of us spirituality comes later in life. In our first half of life or more we foolishly weave a net of fear, worry and ignorance around ourselves until disease and/or lack of health destroys us. We find ourselves bound by chains we have created. What is worse, or more destructive, our misguided thoughts, or our wrong ways of living? We must make changes in our lives now to rid ourselves of things that deaden our spirituality such as anger, hatred, judgment, greed, and selfish thoughts or from inharmonious living.

Before *Kupuna* Hale's[4] passing, I would visit Oahu as often as possible on my summers away from Chiropractic school so we could have the opportunity to spend quality time with each other. She was well known throughout Hawaii and was respected for her knowledge of the Hawaiian culture, its language and history. She wanted me to remember the language as much as possible since I was living on the mainland in the United States. While reviewing the Hawaiian language with *Kupuna*

---

[4] Lydia Hale, known to many as *Kupuna* Hale, was one of many elder Hawaiian teachers in my life, most of which were women. She was from Waimanalo, Oahu and she insisted that I not forget the language of our *Na Kupuna*. We conversed mostly in Hawaiian when we were together.

Hale I was able to help as many of the *Na Kupuna* (elders) in her area with my traditional hands-on skills (*Mana Lomi*®) as my time allowed. As we drove around the village to offer *mana lomi*® or other health remedies we would speak in Hawaiian with each other and discuss all kinds of things. We talked about the old ways versus the modern ways of living, or how the health of the *na kanaka maoli* (Hawaiian people) has changed for the worst since her childhood days. She would ask me what I would do for a particular physical complaint or what kind of foods or herbs I would suggest to help some of the ailments that the Hawaiian elders had.

On one occasion she told me about a recent gathering on Oahu that was for the sole purpose of discussing the concepts and principles of *ho'oponopono*. There were five Hawaiian *Kupuna* panelists including her and about 100 people in attendance. I could tell she was not happy with the outcome of that *Kukakuka* (talking story) by the intensity of her words. She proceeded to tell me that the entire evening was spent discussing aimlessly whether the concept was called *ho'opono* or *ho'oponopono*. *Kupuna* Hale always had a humorous side, and brought laughter and joy to everything she did, but on this particular day there was a serious tone to her voice that made me pay particular attention. She told me "Your work on traditional Hawaiian medicine and bridging the gap to modern health care systems is very important Maka'ala, but don't get caught up with wasted energies of useless discussions. Keep doing your good work and let your actions speak for themselves, and don't get caught up with discussions that go nowhere." Her words of "*pa'a ka waha, hana ka lima*" stood out for me and I carry this motto in everything that I do. This phrase literally means to keep the mouth shut and work with the hands. What she was telling me was action speaks louder than words. Her concern at the time was that there were many "camps" of Hawaiian speakers and non-Hawaiian speakers on Hawaiian healing that had conflicting ideas about the old ways of treatments and remedies. She said sometimes getting too stuck on traditions could stagnate expansion of an idea or a community. She encouraged me to focus on getting the job at hand done without causing separation from others (judgment, anger, jealousy, greed, manipulation, controlling, comparison, perception of inadequacy, etc.), and to think outside of the box. She reminded me that the old Hawaiian ways of living involved doing things in the best interest of the entire village versus all for oneself and that creativity was true intelligence in Hawaiian thinking.

The following are four simple steps using the concepts of *ho'opono*. For it to be effective, however, requires action, clarity and determination. Of course you must first come to the conclusion that disconnecting from any unwanted negative energies is essential for you to move on or to initiate change.

- Sever (*'oki*) the unwanted energetic cord between you and the person, place, or thing.
- Transmute (*loli'ana*) or surround that which you are disconnecting into clear white light.
- Recycle (*ho'ohana hou*) this transmuted energy into the ethers or universe around you. It is like pouring a cup of water into the ocean where it becomes one with the seawater.
- Replace (*kuapo*) the empty energy receptor, which is created when the cord is cut, with the feeling of joy or positive outcome that you would like.

Once you have committed to letting go of unwanted past emotional experiences (getting rid of the onion versus peeling the skins), you will enter into what I call a transitional state of being. Your stories of your past emotional experience(s), as important as they are, are simply just stories. Blaming others, situations or institutions for your emotional experiences or problems are misplacing your responsibilities. By cutting the cord to negative experiences, and thereby entering a transitional state of consciousness, you have begun a very powerful creative process. Even if others may have contributed to your emotional experiences, you still have the power within to change it all. Severing the cord (*'oki*) means what was, no longer is. What's gone is gone, what is lost is lost. You are 100% committed to moving on with your life.

Don't waste your time in anger or sadness. Step into your identity as a creator of your own life. To remain in the past is to lower your state of consciousness. Refuse to waste time with meaningless discussion, which can create a negative vortex that prevents your soul from expanding outward. If you are bold enough to step into your identity as a creator, I have this to suggest:

When you have disconnected from the "onion" that is of no use to you anymore (your perception of a former reality), you have stepped into a "void point" of transition. A void point is an empty receptor within the transition from the old reality into a new one. It is the place of opportunity to change your "blueprint." The empty receptor exists when we complete the four-step concept of cutting the cord to the energy of accumulated negative thought forms (miasm). This transitional place is the so-called, "no-person's land," a term commonly used in the game of tennis. This is that place on the tennis court between the baseline and the service line. You never want to stay there too long because of the difficulty hitting a ball landing at your feet. But it is a place you must enter if you want to reach the net, because being at the net gives you an advantage to winning the match. Therefore, the no person's land is the transitional state of going from A to B.

Transitional states almost always include chaotic times of confusion, despair or fear. However, focusing always on the positive outcome using trust (*na'au pono*), will power (*mana'o pono*) and disconnecting from all doubts, will lead you into discovering the new you.

As a Sovereign Being, you can replace any empty receptor at the void point with a positive outcome reality. You have absolute power of creation and manifestation of your own reality. Be aware however, of what new reality you put into place, for this new reality will become the new perception of your future. So be wise when creating a "new you."

You are now on the path of using the Hawaiian practices and principles to being well.

> *I am love, grateful, happy, healthy, and*
> *financially and spiritually abundant.*

Ho'oponopono Session

Below is an example of an actual ho'oponopono session from beginning to end that I conducted in one of my "Living Pono" workshops. This was similar to how it was done in the old days with my *na kupuna*. This workshop is typically three days long where many ideas and concepts are also discussed.

A middle-aged man, I'll call JJ, presented with a primary focus of "not getting to my highest potential with my creativity." "My intention is to be able to share, for example, my music with others to the best of my ability." My question to JJ was when did you start feeling this way and what do you think is contributing to this? His first response was the description of a car accident he had at the age of 19, which resulted in the person in the other car dying. According to JJ, his pattern since this tragic accident was to point to this event every time there was (a perception of) failure or doubt in his life.

JJ grew up in a non-supportive family and his dad constantly pressured him to study and to excel in everything he did, especially in academics. He pushed and preached excellence in academics throughout JJ's elementary school, high school and college years, but never recognized JJ's accomplishments as an honor student at each level. His mother asked him to play his music from time to time, but always made comments following his performances like, "it didn't sound like the original artist". His learnt behavior of perfection started at a very young age. This behavior later carried over to his daughter, which JJ agreed was a possibility.

Essentially, this is JJ's story focusing around his ability to be creative, especially in music. So where does he start? How does he "connect the dots" to bring some sense into the picture, and how does he find the "onion?" What are the steps for JJ to move on with his life to change the blueprint of his perceived failed patterns on a cellular level?

As a side note, the 'onion concept' is a Western approach of processing inner turmoil, one leaf at a time. The Hawaiian *ho'oponopono* approach is to get rid of the entire onion.

The first thing that was discussed was the car accident that happened thirty plus years prior to his story. This is a long time to hold and carry a heavy burden of responsibility and guilt (something he admittedly expressed).

It was time to *'oki* (sever) the emotional energetic connection to this entire event. This included any thoughts of:

- Not being allowed to the funeral of the other driver.
- Not being allowed to apologize because the parents of the other driver didn't want to see or talk to him.
- The trauma of the accident itself.
- The hospital experience and what his family went through because of this.

After going through the four steps of *ho'opono* it was time to reset the signature of the resulting 'empty energetic receptors' within his energy field of consciousness using a linguistic template reprogramming statement: "I am free to move on with my life."

The next roadblock that needed to be removed was his relationship with his father and mother (both already crossed over to the other world). He needed to let go of the memory of always trying to satisfy them and seeking approval, a behavior pattern that needed to be severed. Finally seeing and feeling satisfied with his creativity without needing the approval of anyone and with no attachment to the outcome. It is interesting to note that the music he creates has received rave reviews by high level music lovers in the U.S. and abroad.

The conclusion of this class session was for JJ to create a positive statement that he could use to remind him of who he is today. "I am expressing my creativity with ease, joy and gratitude."

Notes

CHAPTER 2

Ke Ola Pono
The Principles of Health

Certain fundamental truths existed for the ancient Hawaiians (*kanaka maoli*) that were applicable then and still are today. Accept it or not, there is a Principle of Life within our universe and time construct for all *po'e kanaka* (human beings). All things come from and are made from One Living Substance. This Living Substance is omnipresent and fills the interspaces of all things within our universe. It is a Substance that exists in all things and all life comes from it.

We, as *po'e kanaka*, are a form of this Living Substance and therefore have within us the Source of Health (*Kumu Ola*). It is from this Source of Health that all healing takes place, no matter what modality or remedy is used. However, it is only by thinking in a *pono* (aligned, balanced) way and taking action can we access *Kumu Ola*.

If you believe that a prescription pill will help your ailment then it will. If you believe strongly that herbal formulations will help your ailment then they will. Even within the same system there are differences in treatment that may or may not have a positive outcome. The allopathic treatment for gastric ulcers for example, has at least 5 different prescription protocols, which include two different antibiotics and proton pump inhibitors. Similarly, within the alternative healing system, cayenne, green tea and vitamin supplements may be prescribed. These two healing systems in theory and practice help "cure" most diseases. These two different systems, however, have not been, and cannot be, used effectively at the same time in a sick person. Through observation, one could conclude that it is an internal Source of Health that heals many people, not just the various remedies.

What about the Chiropractor who manipulates the spine, the indigenous healer using the power of prayer, fasting and nutrition, or the Scientologist and his doctrine? What conclusion can we come to from the results that they get? All these modalities and treatments do help people with their ailments, but not without the action of the Source of Health. The ancient Hawaiians understood the power of *Kumu Ola* that exists in all people. They understood how to tap into this potential to accomplish all the cures needed, paradoxically, in a time when canoes were the only mode of transportation from island to island. At that time Hawaiians were ridiculed by the colonial white people as being "savages" and unable to survive without the salvation of religion. Today, it is the medical system that is saying, "Hawaiians need modern medical care if they want to be well."

In the old days the *Kahuna La'au Lapa'au* (medicine master) helped the patient to think about the remedy through ceremony and prayer, rather than just the ingredients in the prescription. A relationship was always developed between all parties involved including family members, plants used and the *Kahuna*. They gave offerings to give thanks for the healing to take place and they cleared any mental obstruction (through *ho'oponopono*) that might hinder the healing process. The *Kahuna* understood that ultimately the healing power existed within each person.

To drive the point home, let me say that the Power that heals exists in all of us, but it is not activated by the physical or mental means used, but rather by the way the person thinks about these. There is a Source of Health in every *po'e kanaka* that is related to this healing power. Thinking in a *pono*[5] way speeds up the activation process.

---

[5] Pono is a concept that means being in balance with the self and all things related to it. It means living in harmony; being attentive to the intention at the inhale breath before exhaling the words from thought; it is taking responsibility with every action produced.

No matter what system of healing is used or what remedies are prescribed, your getting well depends largely on how you think and act for permanent healing to take place. The way people think is determined by what they know rather than what they believe. If it feels right to you then you know it is the right thing to do. Trusting your *na'au* (gut feeling, intuition) results in the strength of the thought as it applies to healing the self.

Generally speaking, having absolute trust in the effectiveness of the treatment prescribed will result in a positive outcome. However, it has been my experience as a Doctor of Chiropractic, and as a Hawaiian medicine specialist, that many people easily have trust in potential treatments for others, but find it more difficult applying these treatments to their own situation when they are not well.

Having *na'au pono* (trust) in being well when treatments are applied affects a positive outcome. It is not enough to just think about healing. You must take action (*ho'o…*) and apply it to yourself by externalizing your thoughts and expressing them in your life. *You must act in the same way you think.* Your *na'au pono* (trust) backed by *no'ono'o pono* (discipline) and *mana'o pono* (will power) for your personal healing are important ingredients for the envisioned outcome. Feel it as if you are living in accordance with the focused outcome, which is that you have a strong, healthy, functioning body.

> *I have a strong, healthy, functioning,*
> *youthful, body, mind and spirit.*

Notes

CHAPTER 3

The Foundation of Na'au Pono
Knowing, Intuition, Trust

Thinking in a *pono* way and trusting your *na'au* based on fundamental truths will cause a disease process to stop or even reverse itself. This fundamental truth is repeated here: All things come from and are made from One Living Substance (*Kumukahi*). All things that we see and feel are made from this formless Substance, and its life and intelligence exists simultaneously in all things.

Much, much more can be said about the Polynesian's original history (ancient stories, chants & songs) than has been revealed within Hawaii and to the outside world. The Hawaiians have the *Kumulipo* chant for example, which is about all things created by *Kumukahi* including *na po'e kanaka* (humans). Other islanders of Polynesia also have their own version of the "chant of creation." Within these oral histories are overlapping layers of hidden truths (*kaona*) that describe all things originating from *Kumukahi*.

There exists within *Kumukahi* an intelligence that creates motion and form from thought. When we see and feel these forms we are experiencing a frequency of light energy that is resonating in different patterns of position and orientation. To explain this further is to think of pixels of light turning on and off in a specific pattern that models a specific form or motion. Let's say that within our three-dimensional reality our conscious mind is interpreting three sets of twelve lights where each set of lights are blinking off and on in a specific speed and pattern. As our conscious mind expands outward into the higher frequency of reality, more lights are available that blink faster then the frequency of the previous level. When our conscious mind reaches the twelfth dimensional frequency and beyond, all of the lights stay on. This is where the past, present, future, (multiphase, multi-dimensional) are seen simultaneously!

When *Kumukahi* wants to create a particular form, it thinks of a frequency of patterns that will produce that form within our reality. When it wishes to create a taro plant for example, it thinks of the sequences of resonating light energy, which results in the form of a taro plant. All thought forms of *Kumukahi* benefits the "whole" and is always done with love, therefore the resulting frequencies are eternal and sustainable. When we create thoughts of energy that benefit all people and are done with love, the outcome becomes eternal. When it is done for personal gain or for the self with no consideration to the "whole" then it is temporary and will not sustain.

The human body is formed from *Kumukahi* and is the result of specific frequency of light energy, which originated as thought from *Kumukahi*. The energetic *mana*, which produces, renews, and repairs the human body, has two forms of function, which modern science describes as voluntary and involuntary functions. Voluntary function of the human body is done in accordance with the conscious will of the individual and involuntary function would be the opposite.

Before going on, let me briefly go over the human bodily functions. The human nervous system is divided into two primary sections: the central nervous system and the peripheral nervous system. The central nervous system, or CNS, consists of the brain and spinal cord. The peripheral nervous system, or PNS, includes all the nerves that are not part of the CNS. The PNS can be further divided into the sensory division, which transmits sensory information; and the motor division, which sends impulses from the CNS to the muscles. The motor division can be further separated into the somatic nervous system and the autonomic nervous system.

The somatic nervous system regulates the movements of muscles under conscious control, such as the skeletal muscles. Any voluntary muscle movement, therefore, is controlled by the somatic nervous system. Once you decide upon an action, your brain sends a signal to your somatic nervous system to perform the movement. Examples of voluntary muscle movement include simple activities like giving a thumbs-up or complex motions like playing tennis or basketball.

The autonomic nervous system regulates activities that are not under conscious control. These involuntary functions include the regulation of blood flow, sweating, digestion and many others. The autonomic nervous system works closely with the somatic nervous system. For example, you use your somatic nervous system to engage in voluntary physical activity, like running. Once you start running, your autonomic nervous system kicks in to speed up your heart rate and breathing, increase blood flow to your muscles and fire up your sweat glands.

The autonomic nervous system can be further subdivided into the sympathetic and parasympathetic nervous systems. These opposing systems balance each other out. The sympathetic nervous system acts to stimulate the autonomic nervous system, such as by increasing your heart rate in response to a flight or fright situation or other physical activity. The parasympathetic nervous system acts to calm down your heart rate once the danger or activity has passed.

In the Hawaiian principles of being well there is an eating, breathing (not to be confused with respiratory rate), drinking, and sleeping aspect of human function, which correlates to voluntary function (*ola pili'ana aku*). Then there is a thinking or thought aspect of *kanaka kuleana* (human function), which correlates to involuntary function (*ola pili'ana mai*).

As long as a person thinks in a *pono* way and eats, drinks, sleeps, and breathes in a *pono* way, he/she will be well. Both aspects of human function are either fully or partly controlled by a person's conscious mind and through the power of *mana'o pono* (the will) he/she can have a strong healthy functioning body. Conscious thought affects the subconscious mind therefore it is essential that a person think in a *pono*, healthy way more often than not.

Every person is capable of creating original thought, but not everyone understands or knows everything, especially when it pertains to being well. Without the proper awareness of life and health, unhealthy or limiting thoughts can lead to disease and abnormal functioning conditions. Believing that we have limited control of our health or that we are prone to disease, eventually distorts the action of the principles of health. This in turn, leads to unhealthy conditions, abnormal functions and ultimately disease.

In *Kumukahi* there are only the thoughts of perfect functioning health, a complete and expansive life. *Kumukahi* never thinks in terms of disease or imperfection. Disease was not created by or bestowed upon the human race by *Kumukahi*. It is a product of individual thought that has caused a separation of consciousness from *Kumukahi*. *Kumukahi*, God, Goddess, *Akua*, etc. (however you choose to identify this Source) does not think disease, know disease, see disease or recognize disease. Disease is only created by the thought of humanity. In *Kumukahi* there is only perfect health.

Death, disease, abnormal functions and illnesses are the results of negative conditioning and programming, which resulted in a generation of people with distorted consciousness. It is this shift in consciousness that helped us to forget what it is to be a balanced human being. To the best of my knowledge and from the history passed down to me from my *na kupuna*, this distorted perception in Hawaii started during the Warrior Period (between 400 AD and the mid-1800's), but may have originated even earlier. The Warrior Period is when the class system of separation was imposed upon the peaceful sovereign original people of Hawaii from the aggressive south pacific warriors. They also forced upon these people the idea that connecting to *Kumukahi* can only happen via the ruling class. Incredibly, this form of limited thought continues today.

Kumukahi responds to the fundamental impulse to create and expand. All things must live and multiply. It is the nature of the Original Source. The natural state of a human being is a state of perfect health and *Kumukahi* is constantly seeking that homeostasis.

Disease does not exist in *Kumukahi* because its purpose is always the expansion of health and perfect living. All *na po'e kanaka* (humans), being a form of *Kumukahi*, have perfect health and always will. It is our subconscious programming that has caused this separation from positive possibilities. The conditioning programs throughout the world come in many forms. The biggest is through media distortion, obstruction in the world of academia, self-proclaimed health gurus and the food industry. Distribution of misinformation about our diet by the health and pharmaceutical industry to boost profits with little care to our health is yet another. An important ingredient to manifesting health then is to break the blueprint to disease by first changing our mental attitude of living in limitation. We have the power within to manifest anything and everything we need for living in balance. Another important ingredient is to not disseminate any negative programming of limitation to our children from the moment they are born. For example, eliminate anything that deteriorates their immune systems such as immunizations and unhealthy food! Learn to use nutritional medicine and natural herbal remedies that work to achieve optimal health at every stage of life and for future generations to come.

Any human being in optimal health is in alignment with the thought of *Kumukahi* and are living their lives in a *pono* way. The following are the basic truths of the Hawaiian principles and practices of being well:

There is a Kumu'ike (Wisdom Source) from which all things are made that exists in all things within the universe. It is where all life comes from.

The thought from this Source shapes the form and energy of all things that are of this world. The form and energy created are always of perfect function and health. If we as humans think only thoughts of perfect function and health then the outcome is perfect function and health. All the Power of Life will be there to assist us in whatever our needs are. The manifestation of this healthy outcome enhances greatly when we take action by living in a healthy and pono way.

The first step therefore is to learn how to think thoughts of ideal health and function. The second step is to learn how to eat, drink, breathe, sleep and live in a perfectly healthy way. When these two steps are taken, a healthy body ensues.

I am one with Kumukahi and Kumukahi is one with me.

Notes

CHAPTER 4

Ola Kino
Our Amazing Body

In the many years that I have been practicing traditional indigenous Hawaiian medicine (my training started at the age of 6), I am always amazed at what the human body can do. It renews its cells every microsecond of each day, it eliminates waste and toxicity, and it repairs itself when there is an injury. Our body is Life. Life is energy and a gift from *Kumukahi*. We do not produce Life within our body. Life produces the body!

Our physical body starts with one cell then it expands into two cells and doubles itself thereafter. Eventually, groups of cells differentiate into different organ systems and body parts. The Life in the human body is not generated by its growing; it is the Life that makes the body grow. Life is first; body function comes after.

So Life differentiates all things made in this world. There is an intelligent energetic force that originates from *Kumukahi*, the Source of Life. This Life Source or *Kumu Ola* is the source of health in everyone. To activate it, you only need to think in a *pono* way and trust your *na'au*. The alignment of thought and trusting intuition along with the outward action of daily choices will positively bring everlasting health. The outside actions must be consistent and *pono* with your thoughts. You cannot expect to have a strong, healthy, functioning body by thinking health while smoking, eating and drinking junk foods, breathing polluted air, or having bad sleeping habits.

The universal Source of Life then is the source of health in all people. Life in the human body, like life in the universe, is made from *Kumukahi*, which is alive. This Intelligence creates all forms of energy by thinking them and all energy forms differentiate into various functions according to its thought.

Ancient Hawaiians understood and knew that *Kumukahi* thinks only health for all its creations. All energy comes from this vital Source, and wrongful thoughts of imperfection could not be a part of conscious truth of life. To have life there must be a health component. *Kumukahi*, which is the all-knowing truth, cannot be of disease because of the state of "vibrational harmonization." It is all about the creation of wholeness and the perpetuation of life, which is always about being well.

The human consciousness within our present dimensional construct has limitations and therefore not perfect, but at the same time it is a form of *Kumukahi*. It is from a limited knowledge of consciousness that we as humans can think of erroneous thoughts in our body. Initially, our limited thoughts may not cause a disease or an imbalanced body, but when our thoughts become habitual by conditioning, or are self-inflicted then the negative results reflect that wrongful thinking.

Repetitive thought from the conscious human mind and equivalent lifestyle habits creates a corresponding condition in our body. Having thoughts of being unable to heal our own body and living in a physically unhealthy way are often consistent with disease. Healthful lifestyle habits such as eating, breathing, sleeping and periodic cleansing of the body combined with a positive mental attitude are important ingredients if we want to be well. Somehow many of us have forgotten how to follow the true knowledge of life and of living in balance.

We have forgotten when, what, and how to eat. We stay up late into the night, which has shifted our rhythm of natural sleep. We are out of tune with the setting and rising sun. We know little about breathing and how it can contribute to being well. We have forgotten how to quiet the mind and have lost the sensitivity of our connection to *Kumukahi* and all things around us. Living has become a matter of reasoning or habit, rather than instinct and intuition, which all animals naturally have. We have lost our instinct to be one with nature. Many of us are just out of touch! A simple test is to look at the sun and its position in the sky. See if you can determine what time of day it is or how many hours are left in the day. Can you calculate when it might rain or when the rain will stop?

We have reached a "tipping point" in our evolution due to wrong ways of living. The only path, which is in front of us, is to begin to make what is wrong right again. This is the path of "living *pono.*" The purpose of this book is to share the many possibilities of rightful living, so that anyone reading it can succeed in having a healthy body. The responsibility is yours.

Thinking and imagining of feeling well and realizing that you are one with *Kumukahi* is part of the manifestation of perfect health. We don't need to only rely on outside means for healing. We just need to remember how to instill those thoughts of health so our true power of healing can be realized.

When we received treatment from the allopathic doctor or the non-allopathic professional, we were also tapping into our abilities to think in a *pono* way and trusting our *na'au.* There is no prescription drug or herbal remedy or homeopathic dose that has the sole power to heal disease. Not even prayers or indigenous chanting! Of course, they appear to help initially, but ultimately the power to heal lies within the power of thinking and acting in a *pono* way making healing a reality.

Anyone who has overcome his/her disease by whatever system, has, at least once, thought in a *pono* way and trusted his/her *na'au.* The absolute feeling of *na'au pono* and the soul level intensity of it can and will change the blueprint from disease to health forever.

There was once a South American medicine man that gave a dog some non-toxic herbal mixture with a secret pinch of deadly curare in it. Curare is a plant that stops the synapses (electrical impulses) between nerve endings, which causes immediate death. Within minutes of this ghastly demonstration, the unassuming concoction shut down the dog's physical functions and death followed. The purpose of this demonstration, although rarely used, was to convince a deathly sick middle-aged woman and her family that if she took the same perceived concoction and lived, the medicine man would be able to help her. Before giving her the preliminary herbal mixture, however, the medicine man secretly left out the curare. Much to her delight and to her family and friends in attendance, she was still alive! Within days of her newly prescribed treatment, her heath returned to normal. This woman (as did the others) had such a strong conviction that she was going to be well that it activated *Kumu Ola* (Source of Health) within her. After the successful herbal preliminary test, she and the others no longer thought about her disease, but instead connected entirely and completely with health. This true story shows one of many ways that our minds are capable of changing the blueprint from disease to health.

The three essential thought processes of thinking in a *pono* way to make you healthy or to maintain your health are, first, deep concentration on the outcome of health by *na'au pono*. Second, *'oki* or sever the unwanted connection with disease or doubt about your heath, and third, reprogram your relationship with health.

Our thoughts affect every cell in our body, which in turn affects our physicality. Dr. Masaru Emoto of Japan showed scientifically how words have a direct effect on water. He had two glasses of water from the same source; one with the word "love" on it and the other with the word "hate" on it. Through a high-powered electronic microscope photographic system, he was able to show pictures of the frozen water molecules. The image of the water molecule with the word "hate" was distorted or disfigured. The image of the "love" water was beautifully & perfectly formed. What is of interest to me is the fact that the human body is made up mostly of water! If you think disease or have constant fear of it then you will cause disease in your body. If you consistently think of having health then that will be your outcome.

Having a deep belief of *na'au pono,* that a prescribed herb or pharmaceutical drug will work no matter what system of healthcare or medicine used will certainly result in a positive outcome.

Na'au pono must be specific to your situation, and more importantly, you must apply these principles to yourself. A strong, healthy, functioning body comes with personal action of thought and applying your *na'au pono.*

> *I have the power to tame my mind, heal my body and connect with my soul.*

Notes

CHAPTER 5

No'ono'o Pono
Discipline

In order to *'oki* our mental conditioning with disease, we must establish a mental connection with health. Our focus is on the positive outcome not the negative. We don't have to force one away, but rather embrace the other.

Severing the thought connection with disease and reestablishing the thought connection with health requires commitment and "taming of the mind." Never accept defeat no matter how long it takes.

The first step in the Hawaiian principles and practices of being well is to totally commit to focusing completely on *ho'ono'ono'o pono* (mindful action) with health. The best way to have complete thought connection with health is to visualize you having a strong and healthy body. To help you visualize, create a positive statement that fits the outcome that you want. For example, "I am strong and healthy." Each morning and evening silently say, "I am strong and healthy" and repeat this 100 times or more with no break in between. This is your mantra for the next two or three months.

In the beginning, just the intention of having a perfectly strong and healthy body is all that is necessary to get the ball rolling. The intention of being well and having a strong and healthy body is essential to forming the concept of a perfectly functioning body.

For many, having a clear image of being well and seeing a strong and healthy body can be difficult especially if there is no idea what that looks like or how it feels anymore. However, it is not essential nor is it necessary to have a clear mental image of yourself, as you want to be. What is important is to form a concept of ideal health and to establish a relationship with that idea. Although a concept is not a mental picture of health, it is an understanding that identifies you as having a perfectly functioning body. Make every thought, action, and the words that you speak, in alignment (*no'ono'o pono*) with the outcome of a strong and healthy person. Everything that you do, do it as if that outcome has already occurred. Imagine the feeling of what that might be. For example, if there is physical labor, imagine the feeling of unlimited energy, of never feeling tired or weak. If there is work that requires mental action, imagine completing all the work in a timely manner, with ease and with joy.

Intention forms a concept, which when applied to the self, leads to a positive outcome.

Intention leads to a *concept* + *applied to*
self = *a perfect functioning body.*

Never put yourself in a position where you feel defeated before you even begin. Lifestyle changes can be very intimidating and overwhelming at first. As often as possible, visualize yourself accomplishing specific tasks with strength and vitality. The more you visualize that outcome, the more the outcome will become a reality.

In the not so distant past (in Hawaiian we say *i ka wa kahiko*), the *Kahuna* practitioners (medicine masters) would often visualize a healthy, functioning person when treating a patient. They also provided appropriate ceremonies and established a positive doctor/patient relationship before offering treatments. In most cases, their objective was to convince the patient that complete healing was the only possible outcome. To further solidify the concept of health, the patient was taught to practice repetitive positive visualization.

When attention is needed on a specific body part or organ, a person does not need to study anatomy or physiology in order to create a mental image of that specific area. It isn't necessary to "treat" a specific organ or body area for healing when using the *Na'auao Ola Hawaii* principles. No matter what cultural background you come from, it is essential to know that there is but one Source of health in all human beings. This Principle of Health has control over all involuntary function (*ola pili'ana mai*) of life. The thought of health, combined with a focus on *Kumukahi*, establishes a connection to the specific body part or organ that requires healing. Don't be concerned about how it is done or its mechanism, but rather intend it to be done. The heart does not have a heart "principle of health" nor do the lungs have a lung "principle of health." The Source of Health encompasses all. Our body parts and organ systems are not separate from each other. When a human egg is fertilized, one cell differentiates into many different functioning parts until it becomes a body, yet each cell originates from the first.

When I was attending Chiropractic school in 1988, I remembered my *Kupuna* telling me, "the modern science you are learning at the University level and in Chiropractic school is considered children's science when you compare it to the knowledge of our ancient Hawaiian ancestors." The fact of the matter is, the less you know of the complex detailed functions and intricacies of the human body, the better off you are. If modern day science really provided all that there is to know, we wouldn't have the health problems that exist throughout the world today. It's my personal opinion that our present day knowledge of health science is inadequate and leads to misinformation. Inaccurate thinking about health and the human body leads to a potentially poorly functioning human body, which can lead to disease.

In the past (maybe it is still done in some countries), surgical removal of vestigial organs from our body such as the appendix, pineal gland and the tonsils was practiced because scientifically these organs were considered to be non-functioning. When these organs became inflamed, surgery to remove them was the treatment of choice and, in many cases, still is.

Recent research is showing that the pineal gland has a specific function that was never understood in the past. The pineal gland is involved in secretion of the hormone melatonin. It regulates endocrine functions, it converts nervous system signals to endocrine signals, it causes feelings of sleepiness, and it influences sexual development. Ancient people called the pineal gland the "third eye" and it was thought to have mystical powers. It contains magnetic material in birds and other animals, which is important for navigation. The pineal gland is a photosensitive organ, and is an important timekeeper for the human body.

Many patients in the past have had one or more organs removed because of erroneous information. The point is we were given misinformation of the possible functions or non-functions in the human body, which we accepted as fact. Misleading information leads to limited outcomes.

We in the health care profession are trained in modern schools of higher learning that have relatively limited information about the human body. Scientifically, much remains unknown about the intricacies, inner workings and processes of the body. The nervous system, for example, still puzzles the neurological scientific community today, despite advances in research in the last 20 – 30 years. We are just scratching the surface of what we know about the digestive system, or how food plays a critical role in health, or how fasting and cleansing can stop and possibly reverse a disease process. In recent years, we've come to recognize the role that stress plays in disease, but we have little knowledge of its mechanism. With so many functions in the human body, we can only theorize about their mechanisms or their full purpose because we still lack understanding. The full function of DNA within the human body is still unknown. As humans, do we really only have two strands of DNA or do we have more? Why is it that we only use 10% of our brain and is our brain capacity related to our DNA strand potential?

Another example of erroneous information leading to adverse outcomes is the scientific criterion that is currently used to determine "clinical (brain) death." Brain death is a legal definition of death that refers to the irreversible end of all brain activity including involuntary activity necessary to sustain life such as respiration and heartbeat. The concept of brain death emerged in the 1960s, as the ability to resuscitate individuals and mechanically keep the heart and lungs functioning became prevalent. Today, both the legal and medical communities use "brain death" as a legal definition of death. Using brain-death criteria, the medical community can declare a person legally dead even if life support equipment keeps the body's metabolic processes working. Recently, however, the medical community is rewriting the criteria due to the fact that many patients have "come back" after being declared clinically dead. Today the Harvard Medical School's definition of a brain-dead individual is that the person has no clinical evidence of brain function upon physical examination. This includes no response to pain and no cranial nerve reflexes. Reflexes include pupillary response (fixed pupils), oculocephalic reflex (a reflex eye movement that stabilizes images on the retina during head movement), corneal reflex, no response to the caloric reflex test, and no spontaneous respirations. So when we look back to the many loved ones that we buried because of the definition of clinically dead, how many of them were really alive? What we thought was right was based on limited knowledge of our understanding of the human body. I am not ridiculing inquiry into understanding the intricacies of the human body, however, mistaken ideas on being healthy can lead to thinking limited thoughts of potential, which can lead to an improper functioning body and possibly disease.

The importance of this discussion is to emphasize that each individual does not need to study the intricacies of the human body to understand how to find health. Thinking thoughts of a healthy body, and eating, drinking, breathing, periodic cleansing and sleeping in an *ola pono* (alignment with health) way, goes beyond theories and conflicting opinions for a healthy body.

I know down to the marrow of my bones that the above statement is true, however, there are certain fundamental truths that we should know about, which will be explained in later chapters. You don't need to research the causes or possible outcomes of your present condition or even the name it is given, but rather concentrate on forming the concept of health.

Think about health and the many possible positive outcomes available to you, such as the ease and joy of physical function, or doing work or play with unlimited energy. Make this thought process (mantra) your concept of a strong and healthy body. Cut the cord (*'oki*) to any ideas or feelings that are not in harmony with the envisioned outcome. When there is doubt about the positive outcome or when ideas related to disease come up, immediately focus on cutting that cord. Then, surround those energies with pure white light and recycle the transmuted energies into the ethers of the universe. Think of the recycled energies like a cup of water being poured into the ocean. The water in the cup becomes the ocean. Finally, return to your positive thought of a strong and healthy, body.

When you think of yourself as being *lokahi* (one, unified) with the concept of health, the omnipresent Substance that saturates every cell in your body is creating motion and form according to the thought. The intelligence of *Kumukahi* will cause your body to be rebuilt/renewed with healthy functioning cells.

Be committed to the thought of having a strong healthy body, never giving in to doubt or the thought of a poorly functioning body. *Onipa'a* (stand firm, be committed) in your *mana'o* (mind, thought) and *na'au pono* (trust) that you have a healthy functioning body and see this outcome. Trust the truth within your *mana'o* and it will become a reality. Your thought affects every cell in your body, creating a blueprint of healthy function. In time it will manifest into physical form. There is no set amount of time that this process takes to become a reality. The stronger you commit to this transformation, the easier it is to tame your mind and guarantee the desired outcome of having a healthy body.

In summary, the intelligence of *Kumukahi* exists in all things and throughout our physical body. Through thought, *Kumukahi* forms a healthy functioning human being. Because we are of *Kumukahi*, we have a mind that can also create thoughts that can manifest into reality. The thought of the physical body controls the functioning of the physical body. A thought from the physical mind that thinks of disease or imperfect function, will cause disease or imperfect function of the physical body. The opposite is also true.

If you have a health challenge, don't overlook the possibility that you may have allowed yourself to think thoughts that manifested into physical form. These thoughts may have originated from yourself or from some outside source that has influenced you in some way at some time in your life. From the time of being conceived, our natural state is one of health. However, we soon acquire false impressions from our parents and from society about life. We may have gone through life with inaccurate and limited imagining of our true potential to always have a healthy body.

I am one with Divine Spirit therefore I am of Divine Substance.

Notes

CHAPTER 6

Na'au Pono
Trust the Outcome

The Hawaiian principle of health requires *na'au pono* to initiate the action necessary to *'oki* our connection with health imbalances and to reconnect with the Power within for optimal health. *Na'au pono* allows us to re-establish our relationship with health and *Kumukahi*.

Without *na'au pono* in health the thought connection to disease is never ending and there will always be doubt. And doubt breathes fear. Having fear of anything will connect your thoughts to that which you fear the most.

Having fear of disease, or doubt in your ability to prevent it connects your thought with disease itself and *produces* the energy of disease. Our *'ike kino* (mind body, DNA structure), which is of *Kumukahi,* will create forms from whatever we think. The strength or creative power of a thought is dependent on the amount of *na'au pono* given to it.

Everyday we are inundated with reminders of the need for outside intervention to treat disease or to keep us healthy. We are conditioned to think that we are limited as human beings and without outside intervention we couldn't survive. Somehow, along the way we have forgotten the true power that exits within every *po'e kanaka* (human). We have forgotten that through the intensity of *na'au pono*, the creative power of thought can form whatever we think, good or bad. Without *na'au pono* we couldn't create positive forms.

Kumukahi, the One Source or One Substance, which is in and of all things, has perfect *na'au pono* in every thought. Its purpose is to create, perpetuate and expand life, not cause deficiencies or limitations. Thoughts originated in *na'au pono* have creative energies and are therefore able to affect function and bring about expansion. If you trust that you will be well, then you will be healthy. If you feel that you will eventually be sick, then you will most certainly develop some disease. *Na'au pono* can accelerate the action of the (Hawaiian) principles and practices of health.

If there is no *na'au pono* in health, there will surely be fear that disease is inevitable. It can be challenging to maintain trust in health because we are saturated daily with the fear of disease everywhere we turn especially in the manipulated media. Without *na'au pono* in health it would be useless to think health because the conviction necessary to change your situation would be lacking. Without *na'au pono* in health, you could think and visualize all day about health, but when that one thought about disease enters your mind, the disease thought takes over. Fear of an unknown, like death and disease, weighs heavily for most people because that is what our society teaches us. Trusting that you will be healthy and that you will live with ease and joy throughout your life may be harder to grasp because of the conditioning to think otherwise. Without the power and intensity of *na'au pono*, doubt overpowers the mind, which leads to fear. The fear of disease outweighs the positive outcome because most of us have not been raised in a society that teaches us how to live differently or how to live in a healthy way. Any doubt about health will lead to the fear of the disease itself.

The successful practice of *Na'auao Ola Hawaii* requires complete *na'au pono* in health. *Na'au pono* begins in knowing that health is the universal truth of *Kumukahi*. You must know and trust that you have the power within to change your condition or situation. Through thought, *Kumukahi* can create, and therefore, through thought, so can you.

Like *Kumukahi*, each person has a mind capable of creating original thought, which is a form of energy. Through thought energy, we can manifest everything and anything we ever need. Our *'ike kino* (intelligence within) is of *Kumukahi*, the Original Source, and a healthy functioning body is determined by the *na'au pono* of our *'ike kino*. By thinking with *na'au pono* of a healthy functioning body, the outcome will be that of a healthy functioning body as long as the external actions of eating, drinking, sleeping, speaking, periodic cleansing and exercising is done in a healthy, *pono* way.

The power of *Kumukahi* is within all of us and its intelligence is constantly thinking toward a healthy-functioning-physical-body. All *po'e kanaka* exists in this unlimited ocean of 'health-power.' The use of this power for health, however, is dependent on the power of our *na'au pono*. This limitless power of health is available to all people as long as it is combined with action and with unfailing *na'au pono*. By applying this action to ourselves, we cannot fail to attain a healthy body, for the power of *Kumukahi* and power within each of us is all the true power that is needed.

The knowing of this statement is a foundation for *na'au pono* in health. Once there is a knowing that health is the natural state of all *po'e kanaka* and that we exist within this abundance of health power and that a healthy body is possible for all, we will never fail to attain optimal health.

Once you realize that disease has no power to affect you and its existence is based on distorted thought, you will know that health is light years ahead of disease. Knowing that health is possible for you and that it is readily attained and that you know how to achieve it, you will have *na'au pono* in health. By practicing with determination, the principles listed in this book, you will have this *na'au pono* and knowledge as the wise, ancient Hawaiians did for generations.

Na'au pono takes practice and requires personal application to have any affect on healing. It is essential to declare health in the beginning and to form some concept being truly healthy.

Never visualize or see yourself as "going to be" or "will be" or "want to be" healthy. These affirmations are future tense and can only promote health as a possibility. Confirm with *na'au pono* that you ARE well and claim it to be true. Watch your words or thoughts and see the present moment of being well. For example, "I am/have a strong healthy functioning body." Watch your thoughts on the inhale breath before you exhale the words or visualization of your affirmation. Be sure it is *pono* with your intended outcome. Observe your alignment of attitude and intention of being well and never contradict the action of being well. Pay particular attention to your physical attitude towards the "I am..." affirmation. That is to say, your physical actions and attitudes should be *pono* with that of a healthy person.

When doubt of health or fear of disease sets in, immediately *'oki* the cord to that thought, surround that severed energy with clear white light and recycle this transmuted energy into the ethers of the universe. Then focus on visualizing the outcome of a perfectly healthy-functioning-body. This practice should be done immediately every time doubt or fear appears.

A very important ingredient – perhaps the highest on the list - in the application of *na'au pono* according to the Hawaiian principles and practices of being well is the attitude or practice of *ho'omaika'i* (gratitude). Always give thanks to *Kumukahi* for what you have or for the health you are enjoying. *Ho'omaika'i* opens room for expansion of love and abundance. It strengthens *na'au pono* and it creates a stronger connection to *Kumukahi*. Each and everyday, morning and night, affirm by saying, "I am grateful for _____"

As a reminder, there is an unlimited flow of life from *Kumukahi* to all things and to all people according to his/her *na'au pono*. Health-power from *Kumukahi* is never ending and each day having *ho'omaika'i* and thanks, brings an abundant of health. Having *ho'omaika'i* daily will help tame your mind by giving you more control of your field of thought. *Ho'omaka'i* deepens your relationship with Source. The more deeply you establish a relationship with *Kumu Ola* (Source of Life) the more open you are to receiving the abundant life from it. In developing this relationship with Source you will realize that it is simply a matter of mental attitude. Our relationship to *Kumukahi* is not a physical one, but rather a heart-mind connection. A person who feels deeply and sincerely with *ho'omaika'i* will be more connected with the One Source than the person who never gives thanks or shows gratitude. A grateful mind receives unlimited flow of health-power.

The vital power of life comes from the One Source, which the (Hawaiian) principles of health are connected to. A person develops his/her relationship with the principles of health by na'au pono in health and by ho'omaika'i for the health he/she receives. This is all accomplished through the proper use of his/her mana'o pono.

I am grateful for the abundance that is before me.

Notes

CHAPTER 7

Mana'o Pono
Will Power

To know truth begins with the mana'o pono to know truth.

You may not immediately recognize when you use will power to know, but you can always initiate the *mana'o pono* to know what you want to learn. If you want to experience true health then you can use your *mana'o pono* to do so. The wisdom and knowledge shared in this book, which was handed down through the generations by the Hawaiian elders (*na kupuna Hawaii*), is the truth about health, and you can use your *mana'o pono* to discover it. Through experience comes the knowing, and experience takes action. This essentially must be your first step toward being well. It is your choice and only yours to make. The truth from the *na kupuna* before us can only be effective if you use your *mana'o pono* to know it.

Apply your *mana'o pono* to the following statements:

- In *Kumukahi* there is intelligence, a Thinking Substance from which all things are made.
- In *na po'e kanaka* there exist the ability to receive the endless flow of the principle of health, which is his/her life from this Substance.
- Each person is a Thinking Substance – a person's thought determines the outcome of her/his health and the functions of her/his body.
- When a person thinks only thoughts of a healthy functioning body, he/she will create a healthy body. This is true as long as his/her external and voluntary actions and attitude are *pono* with his/her thoughts.

When you use *mana'o pono* to know these statements you must also take action to experience them. There is a famous Hawaiian proverb; "*pa'a ka waha, hana ka lima*" – talk is easy, but right action requires work ("action speaks louder than words.") Obtaining the knowing, which is infinite, requires action. The only way to increase the intensity of knowing truth until it becomes *na'au pono* is by taking action in the right direction. Don't expect any positive outcome if for a second you think the opposite is true.

Having *na'au pono* in health requires your action to be *pono* with health. The contradiction of hopelessness felt by a sick person will dim the light of their *na'au pono*. If you act like a sick person you will think like a sick person. If you think of yourself as a sick person then you will forever be a sick person. If you think of failure then you will experience failure.

The first step then is to internally act like a healthy person so that externally you will act like a healthy person. Form your perception of a healthy person; think about a healthy body until it begins to have a definite meaning to you. Visualize yourself as doing things the way a strong healthy person would do them and have *na'au pono* that you can and will do things in that way. *Onipa'a* (persevere) this until you have a clear perception of health and what it means to you.

A perception of health is an idea of the way a healthy person appears and behaves. Continue to connect your thoughts with health until you form a perception of how you do things, how you look, and how you live as a healthy and balanced person. Visualize yourself doing everything as a healthy person would until that connection to health provides the concept of what health means to you. As I mentioned previously, it may initially take some time to form a clear image of yourself being healthy, or impervious to disease, but you can begin to form a concept of yourself as a strong and healthy person.

As you form this perception, think only thoughts of a strong healthy functioning body as it relates to you and, if possible, in relation to others. Any time a thought of sickness or disease enters your mind; do not let yourself get into a mental dialogue about it. Observe the thought without judgment or opinions then let it go. If it comes at you heavy and fast and you are feeling like you are in a "tight spot," resort back to the four-step system of cutting the cord (*'oki*) and the *ho'omaika'i* (gratitude) practice. Connect yourself with *Kumukahi* and give thanks for the abundant health this Source gives you. You will find calmness in your thoughts and you will begin to think what you want to think. "I am a strong healthy and balanced person and I am grateful for the health I am receiving."

'OKI (SEVER) ALL MENTAL CONNECTIONS TO DISEASE AND CONNECT ONLY WITH HEALTH!
It is the key to the path of healing through your heart mind.

Apply your *mana'o pono* to select only those thoughts that support health and organize your immediate surroundings so that they clearly imitate thoughts of health. Eliminate any literature or pictures that convey disease, death, sickly, aging, or physical deficiencies. Display things that depict vitality, health, joy, happiness, laughter and youth. Don't allow anything that suggests disease to exist within your surroundings. Watch comedy movies that make you laugh.

Think always of your perception of health, your *ho'omaika'i* to Source, and your positive affirmation to being well. Always exert your *mana'o pono* to concentrate on thoughts of health. Let me reiterate by saying, think only on health no matter what confronts you, see only health in you and others, direct your attention only to health and control your thought activity by the use of *mana'o pono*.

Don't waste time using your *mana'o pono* to ask *Kumu Ola* for more energy, vitality or power. You don't need to question how specifically health is to be achieved. *Kumu Ola* will supply all that is needed so long as you focus your attention only to thoughts of health.

We can manifest all the health function necessary for our physical body by always thinking in a *pono* way and by being *pono* in our external input. We can think in a *pono* way by controlling our concentration with the use of our will power. We have the choice on what things we use *mana'o pono* to think about.

I am grateful for the abundance of health that exists within me.

Notes

CHAPTER 8

Kumu Ola
Source of Health

This chapter will explain how you can receive health from *Kumu Ola*. By *Kumu Ola* I mean the Thinking Substance from *Kumukahi* where all forms and motions are created. The Intelligent Source that saturates the interspaces of our universe and every cell in our physical heart-mind body. It is where the source of all energy and power springs forth life (*Puna Ola*) that gives vitality to all things. Its only purpose is the perpetuation and expansion of life, which is the expression of its Heart-Mind Intelligence.

By being *pono* (in harmony) with this Intelligence, it can and will give health and wisdom to *na po'e kanaka*. By choosing to take action in living abundantly in a *pono* way, we develop a harmonious relationship with this Source Intelligence (*Kumu 'Ike*).

Abundant life for all is the sole purpose of *Kumukahi*. Should you choose to live more abundantly *pono* then you are establishing *lokahi* (unity) with this Source. By working toward a stronger connection with *Kumukahi*, it will and must work with you.

Establishing a *pono* relationship with this Intelligence requires establishing a *pono* relationship with all people, places, and things. It is essential to want for others what you want for yourself.

By being *pono* with *Kumu 'Ike* you will receive unlimited wisdom and *mana* (lifeforce). *'Ike* does not refer to knowledge of empty facts or foolish intelligence or unsound judgment. *'Ike* is the ability to see truth and the intelligence of how to use this truth in a *pono* way. It is the ability to immediately see what is truly best for you and the collective and how to attain this outcome. With *'ike* you can eliminate wrongful thinking that bring conflict and make clear decisions and choices to meet your particular needs. You will receive guidance through your "higher self" to know how to do what you want to do. By establishing *lokahi* with *Kumu 'Ike*, the all knowing truth and wisdom, you too can and will have *'ike*. Also remember that you must not only establish *lokahi* with *Kumu 'Ike*, but you must also establish *lokahi* with all things, places, and people. If you are unable to consistently bring harmony to all, you will find it very difficult to receive *'ike* from *Kumu 'Ike*. See the highest good for yourself and others. Be grateful and thankful for your life, your body, your mind, and your soul.

Moderation is the key to all areas of life - external necessities for the physical body (food, drink, and physical sensations), necessities for the mental body (knowledge, economic gain, and societal position), and supportive love for others (community service, philanthropy). Excessive attention to any one area over the others causes an imbalance (*pono 'ole*), which is out of harmony with *Kumukahi*. Having excess in one area of life leaves deficiencies in other areas. Wanting health means you want more abundant life, which means you want to be more connected to *Kumukahi*.

So, as you continue on your path as a strong healthy person, stand firm (*onipa'a*) in your desire to live to the fullest in mind, body, and soul and you will gain wisdom. Having *'ike* gives you independence to live your fullest potential towards health.

In addition to receiving *'ike,* you can also receive an abundance of *mana* (life force, vitality, energy) from *Kumukahi*. We naturally and instinctively use this energy, but many of us do not use it to our fullest potential. With intelligence and *mana'o pono* you can increase your power to use this abundant energy. But only you can decide how much of this endless supply of *mana* to utilize.

The ancient Hawaiians understood and knew that since *Kumukahi* has an endless supply of *mana,* so too can all people have an endless supply of power. Through our intelligence and will, we can access the limitless source of power for our mind and body. The Hawaiians of the "pre-warrior period" realized that all humans have unlimited powers because there exists an endless ocean of *mana* from *Kumukahi* that we are connected to. The amount of *mana* we receive, however, depends on us.

The human body when under duress, or in an emergency situation, can have incredible *mana*, endurance and strength - many times more than we realize. Depending on our mindset at the moment, we can summon incredible strength and courage, or we can weaken from doubt or fear.

This was evident when I was co-coaching two Ironman triathletes in the 90's in Kailua, Kona, Hawaii. Endurance, strength, and mental attitude are the key ingredients for a successful outcome in a Triathlon. There are three portions that make up this competition. The swim is 2.4 miles (3.86 Km), the bike portion is 112 miles (180.25 Km) and the marathon run is 26 miles 385 yards (42.195 Km). Usually, it is during the marathon portion of the race when exhaustion (heat & fatigue) sets in. This is the part of the race when the physical body and the mind are really tested. There were external things that I was able to provide to help these Triathletes endure this demanding event. For example, I was able to provide a seawater formulation to help replenish electrolytes naturally, which helps with physical endurance and exertion. I also had them drink a re-energizing drink of water, raw honey and cayenne pepper (*nioi*) to increase blood circulation, which increases oxygen uptake. The one aspect that I couldn't provide, however, was the power within that they needed to draw from, and the willpower to retain a positive (*pono*) mental attitude.

When a triathlete had reached the point of exhaustion and his/her physical strength seemed all but gone, they somehow were able to "recharge" themselves. I knew this firsthand since I ran many marathon races myself in my younger days. Their strength was renewed in an unexplained manner and they appeared to be able to go on indefinitely. This power within went well beyond what I could do for them on a physical level. Depending on the triathlete's mental attitude there seemed to be an "up and down" (like a rollercoaster) cycle of strength and power fluctuation. Each down time they were somehow able to renew the power and strength from within.

To have consistent renewable energy, a triathlete must have absolute *na'au pono* that the strength and power will be there when called upon from within. The mind must continually think of strength and power and have the confidence that he/she has it and can continue to race. This determination allows the triathlete to tap into a source of renewable energy. If doubt enters the mind, exhaustion and physical weakness would almost always be the outcome. When the triathlete stops running, defeat usually steps in and no matter how long he/she waits, the strength and power needed would never recharge in time for the duration of the race.

Similarly, a sick person who has absolute *na'au pono* in health, whose determination and action brings him/her into a stronger connection with *Kumukahi* and who is *pono* with his/her external input, will receive all the *mana* that is needed for the healing of any disease.

The stronger your desire to live life to its fullest potential, the stronger the *Mana* will flow through. *Kumukahi* then begins to strengthen its focus toward you and all that is around you. When you receive it openly with *na'au pono*, it is yours.

The endless flow of *Mana* from *Kumukahi* is given with unconditional love; no matter what deeds an individual has done or has not done in the world.

I am open to receiving 'ike (knowledge and wisdom)
and mana (vitality) from Kumukahi.

Notes

CHAPTER 9

Ho'omana'o
Actions of the Mind

To practice the principles of *'Na'auao Ola Hawaii* successfully, the right use of will and a positive mental attitude are essential ingredients. To accomplish this, you first must recognize and understand that there is an Original Source from which all things are made. Call this Source what you will, however, for the purpose of this book and in alignment with my *na kupuna kahiko* (ancient ancestors), the term *Kumukahi* is used. Within *Kumukahi* there is a *Kumu 'Ike* (Source of Intelligence) that exists inside of us, around us and throughout our universe. All Life comes from this Intelligence, which has an endless resource of energy. *Kumukahi* is the principle of life and the principle of health in all *na po'e kanaka.*

We are thought forms and motions of frequency created by *Kumukahi*, from where we draw an unlimited supply of power and vitality. As *Kumukahi* creates through thought forms, so too can humans create thought forms. We have intelligence within our thought that permeates the physical structure that controls our body functions. If we think consistently of having a healthy body then the outcome will be that of a healthy body.

In order to consciously connect to all possibilities of health, there must be a strong, undying desire to have a strong, healthy body. The stronger our determination is to have a vital body, mind, and soul, the more we are in harmony with the Source of Life. Everything we do must be for the expansion of mind, body, and soul. This will bring us into *lokahi* (harmony) with all that life has to offer.

When we use conscious effort with *'ike*, to manifest all that is needed for our body, mind, and, soul, we establish a deeper relationship with *Kumukahi* and its Intelligence of Health (*Kumu Ola*). This relationship brings an endless flow of vitality and the power to maintain life.

Energies such as doubt, fear, anger, negative mental attitude and selfishness prevent us from receiving the full energetic potential of *Kumukahi*. Any partial disharmony in life disconnects us from the whole, which is to *'oki* (sever) our relationship to the collective. We will still receive energy and maintain life, but never to its fullest potential for our body, mind, and soul. Under these circumstances, our lives can only operate involuntarily and automatically without purpose and intelligence. Our actions and performance with any part of the world around us, affects the harmony, or disharmony, with the whole. "Do unto others as you would have others do unto you." A good practice is to treat everyone and everything equally and lovingly before offering spiritual prayers.

All the positive things you want for yourself should also be something you want for your community

The Competitive Mind

It is very doubtful for someone who has a compromised health to fully recover if he/she maintains a competitive mind versus a creative one. A competitive mind decreases the chances of regaining health because of the mindset of separation. Competition commonly starts at a very young age, through sports and academics and then often continues into the business world. It can lead to ideas of winning at all cost no matter what it takes, regardless of whether it creates harm to ourselves and others, hatred, or jealousy. It is about an idea of "us versus them," which modern society reminds us of constantly. Competition is about the fear of losing and although it can involve team effort, it also plants the seed of separation from the whole. Not only do the thoughts separation create distance between groups or individuals, they also create distance between our spirit and soul and ultimately to *Kumukahi*. Competitive thoughts desensitize our abilities as human beings to be compassionate and loving to ourselves and to one another.

Major corporations, especially in America, have a reputation of focusing too much on maximizing profits while giving little attention to the sustainability of the environment or its resources. Corporate competition is about greed, jealousy and selfishness. It is about taking away the creativity of each individual and the independence it fosters. There are corporate hidden agendas that purposely mislead us to believe that we must rely on them and their information if we are to maintain health or treat a disease (*ma'i*). For example, in 2012, a company called Monsanto was found guilty of false advertising: An advertisement for Roundup that Monsanto placed in Dutch newspapers made a number of misleading claims, according to the Dutch Advertising Code Commission. Earlier in the same year, the Advertising Standards Council of India concluded that Monsanto's claims of economic benefits to farmers from its GM (genetically modified) cotton were baseless. Monsanto has also previously been found guilty of using wrong, unproven, misleading and confusing claims to promote either its GM crops or Roundup by advertising watchdogs in the UK, South Africa and France. Over the years we have slowly broken away from our innate ability to sustain a healthy lifestyle. A competitive mind causes separation from *Kumukahi*, which decrease the potential to find the true power that exists within each of us.

A creative mind taps into the unlimited potential to reach a positive outcome. It can manifest what we want, such as health and love, and can melt away fear. No matter the intentions of any competitive system such as the food, medical or pharmaceutical industries, they cannot prevent a creative mind from being well. We came into this world with a DNA makeup that function in alignment with unlimited potential. The right use of will that is in alignment with the right actions will allow us to tap into the "cup of life". Scientific research is often manipulated for financial gain, and is based on competition for profits rather than the welfare of the people. Confronted with statistics that indicate that disease is inevitable for a certain percentage of the population, one must carefully consider the motivation of the researchers and those that fund them. Never allow a false reality, presented by competitive minds, to convince you that your own health is limited.

Being in the creative mindset allows us to
tap into our Supreme mind.

For some that are looking for health, a positive outcome can be immediate and yet, for others, it may take a little longer. If you are the latter, never allow yourself to feel disappointed. In the beginning, it may feel like you are failing, but with persistence you will achieve the results you are looking for. You will see that you truly have the healing power within. Stay the course (*onipa'a*) to *na'au pono* that the positive results and a bigger and better outcome will unfold.

Ho'o manawa nui: the action of having patience.

Having embraced the fact that you have a creative mind, the next step is to conceptualize that you are in perfect health. Eliminate thoughts that are not in harmony with the concept of having a healthy body. Trust that by thinking only thoughts of health, your physical body will function in a strong and healthy way. Use will power to ensure that your thoughts will be focused only on perfect health.

Eliminate (*'oki*) thoughts of being sick, weak or limited in achieving a healthy body. Do not for a moment think that you are connected to any disease or illness. Immerse yourself and surround yourself with things that represent health and strength. Always have gratitude for all that is provided to you. Feel the power of *Kumukahi* and know that all things are available to you. Rekindle the feeling of joy in your life.

Use your will power of determination in your focus for health in yourself and in others. Do not research, read or speak of disease. When the thought of disease enters your mind, disconnect quickly and immediately move into the mindset of having a healthy body, mind and spirit.

The will power necessary to achieve wellness can be stated simply:

> *Form a concept of having a healthy body and think only*
> *thoughts that are in harmony (lokahi) with that concept.*

Affirming the above statement with *na'au pono, ho'omaka'i* and *mana'o pono* – is all that is required. That is to say – trust, gratitude and a strong commitment to truly live a conscious balanced life is sufficient to achieve any positive outcome. It is not necessary to focus the mind on a specific area of dis-ease. In fact do not think of any part of your body as less than strong, healthy and functional. The power that heals your whole being is the Intelligence of Health within you. Activate your Supreme mind into positive action and *onipa'a* your *na'au pono* in *Kumu Ola* until your positive outcome has manifested.

To maintain a positive mental attitude of trust, gratitude and health, it is essential that your outward actions be *pono* with health. It is contradictory to envision having a healthy body and at the same time be living in an unhealthy way. No matter how hard you focus on health, your actions of wrongful living will eventually lead to dis-ease and sickness. It is important to be congruent with your thoughts, what you eat and drink, the air you breathe and your actions in your daily life. Being in alignment with every thought and every conscious act that leads to a healthy body, mind and spirit will inevitably lead you to that positive outcome. These actions will magnetize the power of life toward health.

The next few chapters will discuss how you may be able to make every act an act of health.

> *I have trust, gratitude and commitment to having*
> *a healthy body, mind and spirit.*

Notes

CHAPTER 10

Hā

The Breath That Contains Mana

One of the most difficult tasks for a soul to go through just prior to leaving its body and just before crossing over to the other side of the 'veil,' is letting go of the breath. Leaving the physical body behind can be a difficult experience. It's a shock when you realize it may be your last breath. Fear sets in because of the unknown, but it is the realization of losing one's breath that gives a person the most anxiety. In life, the function of breathing is obviously a vital one. We can go without sleeping, eating or drinking water for a reasonable period of time, but can only last a few minutes without breathing.

Hā, the Hawaiian word, is more commonly translated in Hawaii as "the breath of life." However, in the field of Hawaiian healing principles, I prefer to use a more descriptive explanation that connects to the whole. It is "the essence of life from which the evolutionary process unfolds." *Hā* contains *mana* and *mana* is the energy that sustains the manifestations of the universe. *Mana* exists inside and outside of us and is the vital force in our body and mind. It flows within every cell in our body and is the most important thing that keeps us alive.

Every particle of the physical body, every DNA, every cell, organ and gland pulsates with *mana*. The heart has a rhythmic beat, the diaphragm expands and contracts, the biochemical fluids flow in harmony by maintaining homeostasis, all due to the pulsation of *mana* in the body.

The breath can be used as the medium of one's spirit and attitude. *Hā* is the key in uniting the body, mind and heart. Your intension on inhalation determines the outcome or attitude of your words or actions on exhalation. Breath then is the energetic essence of action.

Ha not only involves intentions, it requires the physical practice of controlling the breath that involves many sequences of physical, neurological and chemical interactions.

Breathing is an involuntary function that brings oxygen into the body and expels carbon dioxide. In mammals, breathing in is usually an active movement, with the contraction of the diaphragm muscle. At rest, breathing out is a combination of passive and active processes similar to a deflating balloon.

Breathing is controlled unconsciously by specialized centers in the brainstem, which automatically regulate the rate and depth of breathing depending on the body's needs at any time.

While exercising, the level of carbon dioxide in the blood increases due to increased cellular respiration by the muscles, which activates carotid and aortic bodies and the respiration center, which ultimately cause a higher rate of respiration.

During rest, the level of carbon dioxide is lower, so our breathing rate is lower. This ensures an appropriate amount of oxygen is delivered to the muscles and other organs. It is important to reiterate that it is the buildup of carbon dioxide making the blood acidic that elicits the desperation for a breath much more than lack of oxygen.

The purpose of explaining some of the intricacies of breathing is to impress upon the point that breathing is a very involved activity, one that many of us take for granted. Therefore, maintaining health also requires that we take care of the apparatus involved in breathing.

As much as it is an involuntary function you can voluntarily determine what kind of environmental air to be in and how deeply and thoroughly to breathe this air. You can also keep the physical mechanism for breathing in an optimal condition in the same way that one exercises to keep one's other muscles in the body conditioned for a sport or other activity.

There is little debate that performing breathing exercises appropriate for your specific physical, emotional and mental condition can transform your health and your life. If the breathing exercise is inappropriate, however, it can be counter- productive, or even dangerous. Some forms of breath-work to consider are: focused breathing, movement-supported breathing, touch-supported breathing, position-supported breathing, meditation breathing (see chap. 14). It would be wise to investigate several of these and select only those exercises that are appropriate to your specific need. For the sake of this book I will list two breathing exercises that may help the general population. They are: *hā maka'ala* – breath awareness or conscious breathing and *hā ho'opapau* – breath concentration or focus breathing.

Hā maka'ala provides a solid foundation for all other breathing techniques and is by itself, transformational. Conscious breathing exercises can help reduce stress, increase relaxation, and even decrease pain. It is about observing the mind-body dialog without judgment or preconceived ideas of what or how things could or should be.

Observing our breathing experience without judgment or opinions as it pertains to our physical, emotional and spiritual healing can unlock the mysteries of our existence and our true power within. By consciously observing the movements of our inhalation (*hanu i loko* or *hā i loko*) and exhalation (*hanu i waho* or *hā i waho*) without filtering mechanisms or manipulation, we start to develop a relationship of breath to our internal and external existence. The breath contains a rhythm of existence that sustains vital life in all of us.

A simple exercise for *hā maka'ala* is to develop a sensitivity of breath through observation, while at rest, or in a relaxed position. This should only be done fifteen to twenty minutes at each sitting. As you gain experience with breath during these short periods of quiet observations, you can then start to observe your breath naturally in other conditions such as a stressful or an emotional encounter. The more aware (*maka'ala*) you are under these various circumstances the more you will transform the way you handle or operate under stressful or other difficult situations in your life. That is, by learning how to follow and observe your breath and how it is related to your thoughts, emotions and physical self, you become more aware of how you react to these conditions.

Awareness of breath, can lead to a more positive outcome in life therefore, breath is the bridge to health and longevity.

Hā Maka'ala

Sit quietly in a chair, a couch or on a cushion on the floor and close your eyes. Put your hands and arms in a comfortable position in front of you or on your lap. Observe and sense yourself sitting and breathing without taking any action. Use your internal sensory abilities and listen quietly without mental distraction to anything inside and outside of you. Pay attention to your physical senses, the coolness or warmness of the air flowing through your nostrils. Is there more free flowing air in one nostril than the other? Sense your weight on the chair, couch or cushion under you. Do you feel more weight on one side of the gluteus muscle group than the other side? How do your shoulders or other body parts feel as you naturally breath? Is there more tension in one area than another? Can you allow yourself to let go?

Notice what is moving in your body as you naturally breathe in and out. If your thoughts start to interfere by judging how you should be breathing, just observe these thoughts, but do not hold on to them. Let it move through you without attachment. Simply be aware of these thoughts and then allow them to leave you. Do not take any action from your overall observation of your body, mind, and breath. Once you are ready, stop your exercise and remain sitting for a few minutes longer and enjoy your relaxed breathing and relaxed body.

For the rest of the day, observe what your breath is doing, but don't try to change it in any way! Allow it to naturally take its course. Through observation, you start to pay attention to how the body and breath are interconnected, which helps you to control the emotions associated with breathing. Is it speeding up while you are having a stressful moment? Are you tensing your body or body parts, or are you holding your breath? Eventually, you will automatically alter your breathing towards a positive outcome that will be healthy for you.

Hā Ho'opapau

Focused breathing is a great tool to further assist you in bringing function and health to a particular area of your body. Through our sensory perception or attention through observation of a particular area of the body, we develop a deeper relationship or sensitivity to the area we focus on. Through our intentions to bring health and function to a particular area, we direct the energies and movement of our breath to that particular area. Envisioning a positive outcome helps as long as there is a feeling associated with that outcome. Feel as if the body part or area is already healthy, strong and functional. If you have trouble feeling this outcome, just set the intention for you and it will lead to a concept or idea, which leads to a positive outcome.

You don't need to force or change the rhythm or depth of your breath. Allow the inhalation and exhalation breath in its natural rhythm to focus and direct itself to the body area of interest. Inhale into the area and exhale out of the area. This is all done without force or effort.

In learning *hā ho'opapau* to assist with health and function, the first step is to learn to be attentive to your senses within specific areas of your body. Scan and sense your body for tension or restriction and observe your breathing patterns. Now, place yourself in a quiet and comfortable position and without physical effort, direct the energies and movement of your inhalation breath to the area of interest. During exhalation, release all tension associated with this area and leave behind a relaxed body part or area. Do this for about fifteen minutes or until positive changes occur, whichever is first. This technique for example, will help a tight neck to let go of tight muscles caused by stress. It will help your arm to uncoil tight muscles from overworking on a computer. There are unlimited possibilities of what you can do for general aches and pain. As with most things, practice brings results, so persevere until your positive outcome is realized.

Ha, when used correctly, can open the crystal seals of a soul and reawaken it from a deep sleep. It is through exhalation that one can channel the essence of *Kumukahi* into all parts of the human body and soul. The producer can manifest healing into another person; download trillions of gigabyte information into another, or assist an individual to tap into the secrets of the Universe.

When auntie Margaret[6] was eight years old, her grandfather (a *Kahuna* from Kona, Hawaii who specialized in *Ha-Ha,* which today is equivalent to a medical intuitive) performed the Hawaiian ritual of *hā pule* with her. This is where the intention of the breath along with a specific chant connected to *Kumukahi* is used to help wake the deep consciousness of a person and/or to download information into the physical memory of that person. Auntie's ceremony, which lasted many hours, consisted of breath work on specific areas of her body and chanting that seemed to go on forever. It is a ritual used to assist the soul in self-awareness and its deep connection to *Kumukahi.* This was the last time a *hā pule* ceremony was ever performed in Kona, Hawaii to my knowledge.

---

[6]   Margaret Machado was one of my Hawaiian healing teachers for 16 years. She lived her talk and embodied the Hawaiian healing principles handed down from many generations before her.

In general, it is essential to remember to breathe fresh clean air. If you can't change a polluted environment around you, then you should leave that environment. If you live in an area where the air is not fit to breathe or if your living space (house, apartment) is not properly ventilated, move. If you work in a place where the air is bad, get another job. Every breath of fresh pure clean air carries life for the body and mind just as food does. Every breath of toxic air, and this includes second hand smoke, shortens your life. You may not feel the immediate ill effects when breathing toxic air, but over the long haul disability is sure to follow.

I am grateful and thankful for the pure fresh clean air.

Maka'ala Yates

Notes

CHAPTER 11

'Ai Ola

Healthy Eating

Unfortunately, most of us are not at a point in our lives where we can survive without eating, drinking, breathing, and sleeping. We are not able to build and maintain a perfectly healthy body through the power of the mind alone or through the unconscious or involuntary functions independently. Therefore, there are certain positive habits that have a direct and immediate relationship with the sustainability of life itself.

No matter how strong or focused a person's thought or mental attitude is, life cannot continue in a healthy way unless you eat, sleep, breathe and drink in a *pono* way. More importantly, there are challenges to living optimally if one performs these functions in a *pono 'ole* way. It is therefore essential that you educate yourself and take responsibility by learning how to carry out these voluntary functions that promotes health. The first and most important step to optimal living is to start focusing on the way you are eating.

Hippocrates, who was born in 460 B.C., was a pioneer in disease and its causes. He believed that nature was the healer, but the patient had to be an active participant. "Let your medicine be your food and your food be your medicine," is his most famous quote.

For years, we have been conditioned to believe that only doctors can discover the cause of sickness and only they are qualified to treat us. We have bought into the idea that only doctors can guide us to a healthier lifestyle, to reverse disease or prevent its recurrence. Call it science or call it medicine. I call it pharmaceutical control to promote drugs--their drugs. If modern medicine saves lives, why are we a nation (U.S.) that is so unhealthy? According to data from the World Health Organization in the year 2000, the U.S. ranked 37th in the world's health systems. That means the U.S. was behind Saudi Arabia, Morocco, Chile, and Costa Rica for its ability to care for the health of its citizens. For a highly developed country, the U.S. was in last place in preventable mortality in 2002-2003.

Allopathic or "conventional" medicine, for the most part is about making a diagnosis and treating a disease with drugs. The medical establishment artificially produces a condition in the body that will drown out any potential for disease or illness to survive. If you have enough antibiotics in you, you will not have strep throat, skin rash, Lyme disease, or whatever. This so-called modern medicine is based on the paradigm of find-the-germ-and-kill-it. What about improving the power and function of the immune system so the body can do the job itself without the drugs that have toxic side effects? We have to look at the motivation of huge profits for doctors and for big pharma. The oath that each medical doctor takes in the U.S. includes *"primum, non nocere"* (first do no harm). Yet, according to the Nutrition Institute of America, "conventional medicine is the leading cause of death in the U.S. (research paper: Death by Medicine, www.leforg)."

I have included some brief medical and health stats that I have researched during Chiropractic school and updated from some of the online medical watchdogs so they can hopefully make you more aware in order to make well-informed choices for your life.

The Nutrition Institute of America is a nonprofit organization that has sponsored independent research for the past 30 years. In a recent study based on extensive research, they have concluded that conventional medicine is America 's number-one killer. Over 700,000 Americans die each year at the hands of government-sanctioned medicine, while the FDA and other government agencies pretend to protect the public by harassing those who offer safe alternatives.

A definitive review of medical peer-reviewed journals and government health statistics shows that American medicine frequently causes more harm than good.

The total number of deaths caused by adverse drug reaction in the United States is about 106,000 per year. The total number of deaths caused by medical error is about 98,000. The total number of deaths caused infection is about 88,000. The total number of deaths caused unnecessary procedures is about 37,136. Add to this some of the other categories like bedsores, outpatient surgery related deaths, and malnutrition, the total number of iatrogenic deaths—that is, deaths induced inadvertently by a physician or surgeon or by medical treatment or diagnostic procedures— in the US annually is 783,936. By contrast, the number of deaths attributable to heart disease in 2001 was 699,697, while the number of deaths attributable to cancer was 553,251 (U.S. National Center for Health Statistics. National Vital Statistics Report, vol. 51, no. 5, March 14, 2003).

The number of people having in-hospital, adverse reactions to prescribed drugs is about 2.2 million per year. The number of unnecessary antibiotics prescribed annually for viral infections is about 20 million per year. The number of unnecessary medical and surgical procedures performed annually is about 7.5 million per year. The number of people exposed to unnecessary hospitalization annually is about 8.9 million per year. [1]

Because many doctors fail to teach their patients about preventative habits, many people have resorted to self-help books and Internet sites for their own remedies. Today more and more people are becoming aware of nutritional and biochemical imbalances that lead to diseases. Many are taking responsibility by educating themselves so they can break the blueprint of unhealthy imbalances. People are also becoming increasingly aware of the need to find the right diet for themselves, but many are not sure what specific changes are needed and how to implement them.

The Anatomy of Digestion

Scientific and medical researchers today, the ones that truly care, are starting to understand how the digestive system plays a critical roll in life and death. It is an understanding that my ancestors knew all too well. All of my teachers expressed the importance of taking care of the *na'au* (digestive tract) before administering herbal and nutritional remedies through some form of cleansing or supervised fasting. "The *na'au* is the foundation to health," Auntie Margaret would always tell me. In my studies with iridology, I have found this to be true. Many conditions in the human body can be traced back to the function or non-function of the small and large intestines. I have seen so many people turn their lives around and recover from ill health as a result of supervised fasting and cleansing focusing on the small and large intestines.

Understanding the basic fundamentals of the digestive tract may help you to understand some of the complexities of this system so you don't abuse it. The sight and smell of food triggers the salivary glands in your mouth to secrete saliva, which contains the digestive enzyme amylase. Chewing helps breaks down food into smaller particles in preparation for stomach digestion. The stomach mechanically mixes the particles of food and secretes various substances such as hydrochloric acid (HCL). HCL helps to digest proteins, fat, vitamins and minerals. HCL also helps to kill bacteria, viruses and parasites.

The small intestines (*na'ana'au*) and pancreas secrete enzymes to help digest and absorb carbohydrates, fats and proteins. The gall bladder secretes bile salts into the small intestines to help digestion and absorption of fats and the fat-soluble nutrients such as vitamin A, D, E, and K. The small intestines are the primary organ in the digestive system involved in the absorption of nutrients. If anything interferes with the secretion of bile salts and enzymes or the absorption process of the small intestines, it may result in vitamin deficiencies and fat mal-absorption.

The function of the large intestines (*uha*) is to absorb water, electrolytes and a few vitamins as well as storage of waste products. At this point, most of the nutrients from digested food have already been absorbed leaving indigestible fiber and water. The fiber intake for the most part determines how long it takes for food to pass through the colon. Mucous is also secreted to protect the cell wall lining the colon from bacterial toxins and physical trauma.

One of the fundamental preventative measures to staying healthy are periodic fasting or cleansing followed by eating wisely in a way that is appropriate for your body type. How and what you eat determines how your body functions and look.

Eating

One of the tools available to help guide us to eating the right foods is our sense of smell. Our sense of smell will tell us what is good and what is bad for our body. Our sense of smell tells us if a food is good enough to eat and our sense of taste confirms it. The cells of the olfactory and gustatory sense organ are connected to the brain, which is saturated with blood that is part of the body's circulatory system. The receptive cells of the brain act as electron probes in the blood to detect what is needed for the body especially to help maintain homeostasis.

There is an incredible amount of information available today, especially on the Internet as to when to eat, what to eat, how to eat and how much to eat. Much of this information is controversial. There are the high protein/low carbohydrate diet, high carbohydrate/low protein diet, vegetarian, vegan, fruitarian, paleo diet, four food group guidelines, lacto-ovo, raw versus cooked or processed, proper food combination, etc., etc., etc.

To say there is confusion is an understatement. Yet all the controversy is unnecessary. The right way is simpler to find than you might think.

You only need to consider the principles which govern all positive or focused outcomes, whether health, wealth, or happiness.

> *Take action now, no matter where in the world you are; let*
> *each individual action be in alignment with your focused*
> *outcome, and put the power of na'au pono into every action.*

For example, if you want to lose weight then start now, whether you are in the city or the countryside, in New York or Tahiti. Educate yourself on the right foods and exercises for you, and then apply the right mental attitude in everything that you do to accomplish this outcome. Having trust that you will reach this outcome takes practice; so trust that every little appropriate step is a step closer to your outcome.

Hunger versus Appetite

It would be helpful to understand some of the processes of digestion and assimilation and the hunger mechanism. Generally speaking, hunger is the physiological need for food. Appetite is the psychological desire for food.

Some of the signs of hunger are stomach rumbling, light headedness/ dizziness, low blood sugar, etc. Appetite is driven by outside influences affected from past experiences or learned appetite – smell of food, social situations around food, and sometimes initiated from your mood. Eating not caused by hunger is an appetite response. Appetite is a result of habit, the meal hour, or the results of odors, taste or sight of food that tempts the desire to eat.

Whenever food is needed and can be utilized by the body, there is a triggering mechanism that stimulates the hunger sensation. This hunger sensation is your cue that it is time to eat. When there is no hunger sensation it is unnatural and wrong to eat no matter how strong the desire or how much one appears to need food. No matter what the condition or state you find yourself in, if there is no hunger signal there won't be the optimal condition (energy or power) to digest and assimilate foods. Without optimal conditions the body cannot use the food in a natural physiological way.

Food, when consumed without the sensation of hunger will be partially digested and assimilated because that is what occurs when food is forced into the body. If food is habitually consumed without the signal of hunger the digestive abilities diminish considerably and are compromised, which sets up an unhealthy situation over time. In my many years as a clinician, I have seen many cases of pronounced digestive and metabolic issues. This diagnosis is correlated with a complete health history compilation that I compared with the reading of their eyes (iridology). Of course there are many reasons why this happens--eating junk foods and drinking chemically made soda water are causes--but often it is because of food being consumed when there are no hunger signals.

You don't need scientific evidence to know when to eat and when not to eat. It is a normal healthy practice to eat when you are hungry and an unhealthy habit to eat when you are not hungry. Therefore, always eat when you are hungry and never eat when you are not hungry. This is being in-tune with Nature, which is being in-tune with *Kumukahi*, which is being in-tune with the pulse of life.

Hunger is the neurological signal of the sub-conscious mind that the physical body needs materials and energy for repairing and renewing the body and maintaining temperature equilibrium. Hunger is never triggered unless there is a need for cellular material and unless there is digestive strength when food enters the stomach.

Appetite is a desire for the gratification of sensation. An alcoholic has an appetite for alcohol, but he or she cannot have a hunger for it. A person in-tune with his/her hunger sensation is never hungry for candy or sweets. The desire for these things is an appetite. You cannot hunger for spiced foods, tea and coffee or other taste tempting foods. If there is a desire for these things, it is with appetite not with hunger.

Hunger signals are Nature's way of telling you the body needs chemicals and other elements to build new cells, to create enzymes when necessary, and to create more energy when needed. When our body is in tune with Nature, it will never call hunger into play if the body has no physical need for food.

Appetite for the most part is a matter of habit. When you consistently eat or drink at a certain hour especially if you eat sweetened or spiced and stimulating foods, the desire will be triggered at that same hour. This habitual desire for food should never be mistaken for hunger.

Hunger does not appear at a specific time of day. It only comes when work, exercise or mental activity requires additional energy or raw materials to rebuild or repair the body. For example, during our four-day Hawaiian fasting program, it usually takes two to three days before the idea of eating subsides. By day three or day four, most participants lose the desire to eat. In fact, many have more energy than before they started the fast. When there is no physical demand or mental energy expended there is no major need to eat food. Mind you, fasting participants are taking in herbal formulations along with grape juice to assist the cleansing process.

Hunger is not something that occurs at specific times of the day or night. It only comes when the body signals the brain that there is a need for nutrition (raw materials). This again is because some form of work or exercise has taken place and the body has used significant amount of energy and internal physiological demands that warrants replenishing raw materials to maintain homeostasis. It is also a fact that if you eat sufficient amount of food on the preceding day or evening, it is not physiologically feasible to have a genuine hunger when waking the next morning. This is especially true if it was a refreshing, restful sleep. During a restful sleep the body is recharged with vital energy and the assimilation of food is somewhat complete. The harder-to-digest foods like meat and pork may take more than 24 hours (sometimes days) to be completely broken down and assimilated, however. The body has no need for food immediately after sleep unless the person went to sleep in a state of starvation. It is not physiologically normal to have a genuine hunger when first waking in the morning even if you are an athlete. I have co-coached two Ironman triathletes in Hawaii in the 90's and it was amazing how much they could eat during the day! However, none of them woke the next morning with a strong hunger for an early morning breakfast. It is just not a normal occurrence and it is not how the body naturally operates.

The early morning breakfast for the most part is only to satisfy a habitual appetite, not to satisfy hunger. No matter how much demand you put on your body, how hard you work or exercise, or even how much you are exposed to the elements, unless you go to bed starved, its not normal to wake with a genuine hunger.

Sleep alone normally does not cause hunger; usually some active prolonged form of work (physically or mentally) does that. One could argue that in dream state it is possible to expend mental energy, but realistically speaking, it is the active wake state of activity that expends the most energy. It doesn't matter who you are or what you do, a desk jockey (a term I use for people that work in an office setting) or a professional athlete; the only plan for you is the no early breakfast plan. It is the right plan for everybody because it is based on the universal law that hunger never comes unless the body demands it. I know there are some out there that are traditionalist when it comes to their 'best meal of the day,' breakfast. They feel that they will be working so hard that day that they can't and will not start the day unless they have their "traditional" breakfast. No matter what the justification presented, when you view the facts on hunger, there is only one solution you will find. No early morning breakfast plan! Let your work revolve around your body's natural biorhythms of eating when hungry not the other way around. The early morning breakfast partly came from the early morning work schedule that the industrial revolution created. You almost didn't have time to eat naturally! The indigenous people throughout the world followed a very simple universal law of hunger. As hunter-gatherers, they ate only when they were hungry.

Many that enjoy their traditional early morning breakfast do so partly to satisfy a habitual appetite and not because the body is signaling the brain that nutrition is needed. The indigenous people of the not-too-distant-past lived according to the natural cycles of nature and were able to function just fine without an early morning breakfast. For many of us, it would be wise to do the same, as we will be far better off for doing so, hunter-gatherers or not.

If you are to live according to the Hawaiian Principles of Being Well, then you should practice never to eat until your body has a genuine hunger. The question you might ask then is, if I am not to eat first thing in the morning then when should I eat my first meal? For me personally it is around noon, but it is something that should be appropriate to you. Noon can also be a more convenient time, but again it should be based on your genuine hunger signals.

Although the human body does most of its repair and growing work during a restful night of sleep and that it is physiologically possible to develop some hunger, it is rare to require food first thing in the morning. There are some people that need to have frequent smaller meals due to their condition or some other parameters that require having to eat something earlier than near noon. Also, if you are doing heavy physically demanding work then you will have a hunger that justifies a good-sized meal. If on the other hand your workload is light then you may have a hunger for a moderate-sized meal. So meal size should be directly related to energy output. As far as when to eat, however, the best general rule of thumb for most people is to have their first meal when they are hungry and not because it is convenient or out of habit. Learn how to pay attention to your body with the mindfulness of gratitude, trust, intuition, and love. Eliminate any habit, fear, anxiety, or social customs and focus on your personal sensitivities to what's right for you.

How And What To Eat

The following are suggested ideas of how and what to eat. They will also give you some idea of how eating in a certain way can and will help break the blueprint to disease and illness. Remember, these are just guidelines for you to follow. As always, you should seek a professional health consultant for help in any specific health compromise you may be experiencing. The goal here is to help you make your own informed decision on preventative health care.

The vast amounts of information available today on how and what to eat can be overwhelming to say the least. We have not reached any conclusions on vegetarians versus meat eaters, cooked versus raw food, low protein versus low carbohydrates, no grains versus sprouted grains, low or no fats versus raw fats and so many other schools of thought. There is insurmountable evidence and argument for and against each special theory, but if we depend on these professionals (scientists, medical professions, PhDs) we will have to wait till the moon turns purple before we absolutely know what the natural foods of humans are.

The most disturbing factor for me in all of this is that I am seeing more and more problems with metabolic and digestive disorders. This usually indicates that people with these disorders are not receiving all the essential nutrients and energy that their bodies need. For example, just because you are eating your daily recommendation (USDA guidelines has always been questionable for me) of protein and calcium, it doesn't mean you are actually receiving that amount of protein and calcium that your body can utilize. If your metabolism is low, it is more difficult to assimilate the foods you eat and more difficult to break down the food into chemical elements that your body needs. Not optimally utilizing the foods that you eat can lead to weight and health disorders. There are a number of factors that can lead to decrease in metabolism--attitude, stress, fast paced lifestyle (eating on the run), quality of food eaten, not being present while eating (multitasking), happy eating versus guilt or shame eating, and many other significant reasons.

A healthy digestive system leads to a healthy body and mind. A healthy digestion can break down foods into molecules small enough to travel through the membrane wall into the blood stream and cells. When the digestive system fails to breakdown the food appropriately, fermentation takes place, which becomes toxic. Toxins are then released into the blood stream, cells and organs, which can lead to illness and disease. Since the digestive system uses more energy than any other bodily function in the body, it is important to have proper digestion to conserve energy. For good digestive abilities, don't overeat, eat appropriate amounts of fiber, fruits and vegetables, and avoid stimulants like caffeine, alcohol, tobacco and sugars. Eat lean grass-fed meat if you have to eat meat, keep hydrated and eat organic yoghurt to help the flora in the large intestines. Goat whey helps the stomach's digestive abilities and alfalfa capsules/tablets help to restore function to the large intestines.

A general rule of thumb when it comes to the question of what to eat is to eat what Nature provides in the environment you live in. *Kumukahi* has created an abundance of perfect foods for all humans for infinite health. *Kumukahi* has also given every person the physical and mental abilities to know what foods he or she should eat and how and when he or she should eat them.

Whenever scientists or biochemical engineers attempt to "improve" Nature, things tend to go wrong. We don't need to recreate the wheel, as they say, when it comes to finding the perfect food. Nature is a physical expression of *Kumukahi,* operating according to the rules of *Kumukahi,* with the energy of *Kumukahi.* Nature provides every person exactly what is needed for perfect health. The highest form of this perfect food can be found in the environment you are living in, which are foods that are best for the requirements of that climate. The foods from your environment will be the freshest, therefore containing the highest life force of *Kumukahi*. By focusing mostly on foods from your environment that has been cared for in alignment with Nature and Mother Earth, a person can be in highest association with the Principles of Life that created them. Therefore, you only need to investigate and learn what foods grow and live where you live.

Now you might ask, which of these foods that grow in my environment should I eat? Does it matter what age, gender, and ancestry I am? What about my condition of health, my daily exposure to cold or heat, and my physical and mental activity? Again, *Kumukahi* through Nature provides a variety of foods in every zone on this planet for all humans. Also, we have all been provided with the ability to know hunger and to taste and to smell so we can find all that the body needs.

Every person needs food as a source for nutrients for the Principles of Health in his or her body to direct the necessary functions for the body and mind to live. Food is needed to provide energy, heat, defense, and tissue repair and growth. Specifically, our body needs carbohydrates, protein, fats, vitamin and minerals, which are found in the flesh, organs, and bones of land and sea creatures. It is also found in stems, leaves, flowers, seeds, grains, nuts, fruits and vegetables from the land and water plants. All humans have been given the ability to discover ways of gathering and preparing foods, which is enhanced when we are in tune with Nature and our bodies. A person's own Principle of Health guides his or her hunger and taste to the particular foods that the body needs at that moment in time. Most young children that have not been disconnected through conditioning will intuitively select exactly what their body needs when presented with a table filled with mixed fruits and vegetables.

In every climate zone, all indigenous tribes of the past had learned over thousands of years, the wisdom of nature and the best ways to gather her food. They had also learned to prepare, and to eat the foods from their specific regions. They did this in perfect harmony with the seasons and cycles of Nature. There is an abundance of evidence showing that many of these people had perfect health, strength and endurance, perfect eyesight and teeth, longevity, mental development, and overall wellbeing. More importantly, they had learned the secrets of healthy living, reproduction, and social behavior. They lived and created a sustainable community of support and exchange of all resources. In Hawaii this community was called an *Ahupua'a*. Research has shown that these ancient "hunter gatherers" exceeded RDAs (recommended daily allowance) two to ten fold (O'Keefe Mayo Clin Poc. 2004 Jan; 79(1): 101-8) depending on the nutrient. These ancient HGs knew more about eating for optimal health and vitality then modern scientist and doctors. The HGs diet has more nutrition than the American Heart Association diet, more nutrition than the American Diabetes Association diet and more nutrition than the USDA food pyramid diet.

What were the secrets of eating for these perfectly healthy people?

- They ate only foods that occurred in nature from their environment or that could be made simply from nature.
- They ate only the best foods and parts of foods that had the greatest nutrient content.
- They ate both animal and plant foods, which were often eaten raw although today eating raw fish from the Pacific Ocean, may not be advisable.
- Dairy products were eaten, especially by-products of milk taken from vital and healthy animals that were well fed on fresh growing spring grasses. (Note: Casein, a protein in cows' milk, has been known to be associated with many health problems in the U.S. I suspect this is because of the genetically modified beef and cow and what is fed to these animals).
- In Polynesia, sea creatures were the primary source of animal food. Fish and sea vegetables were a rich source of nutrients. There was also the fishing *kapu* period when the ocean was closed for harvesting food so it could replenish itself. To prepare for this period, many sea vegetables and creatures were dried in a way that preserved its nutrient content.

- Polynesians had a lot of taro, raw coconut milk, yams, sweat potato, and raw sugarcane.
- Where foods were not growing year-round, some were preserved in ways that maintained their nutrients.
- Agricultural lands were replenished with natural substances like compost and seaweed tea and allowed periods of rest.
- Grains were eaten whole or ground immediately before use. Many grains were also sprouted and eaten raw.
- There were times of natural decrease in food supply and ceremonial times when tribes ate less food or none at all.
- Indigenous people actively participated in growing, gathering, fishing, hunting and preparing their food. They had community ceremonies of gratitude and celebration. Hawaiians called this period "*Makahiki.*"

Polynesians were some of the healthiest people in the world until the *ipu kea* (white people) arrived with unnatural foods and belief systems that contributed to the demise of the native people. They developed disease, deformity, tooth decay, misery, and unsociable behavior. These unnatural foods included refined and chemically preserved foods that were filled with sugar and flavors to hide the absence of nutrients. There were foods from unhealthy plants and animals that fed into the disease and weakness that they developed. Today, for example, there is more Spam sold in Hawaii then all the other U.S. states combined. This is the classic example of denatured food leading to a society of disease and weakness.

What is needed for ideal health is vital food, packed with life force, eaten according to the Practices and Principles of Being Well.

To incorporate these practices into life with vital foods, each person must align himself or herself with the Principles of Life with gratitude and knowing that there is abundant food filled with life force for all. Trust that you will be guided to the best food source available in your area. In the Hawaiian *ahupua'a* system, each person lived in perfect relationship with the Source of all food with *ho'o na'au, ho'o maika'i* and *hau'oli*. They planted and gathered their food with the attitude of sharing with all.

If you don't have the ability to grow, gather and raise your own food, then form a community of friends and family who do. You should choose people who live in harmony with Nature and have gratitude, joy and wisdom in all that they do. A very successful system, especially for city dwellers, is the Community Supported Agriculture Program (CSA). This is where you pay a monthly sum for weekly delivered consciously grown food.

Once you have the sources of a variety of vital foods from which to choose, eat what your body wants. Re-tune your body to the Principles of Health to create infinite ideal health. Have a genuine hunger before eating, taste the food while chewing, and slow down when eating. When done properly, you should feel energized and satisfied. There shouldn't be tiredness, irritability, congestion, or any discomfort (as in overeating). When eating according to your body and in perfect relationship with *Kumukahi*, you will feel energetic and have a genuine feeling of being well over a period of days, weeks and months following your new change. This is how you will know you are eating the right foods for your body. Over a short period of time you will start resonating with life and your new lifestyle automatically without having to think about it. When you re-learn how to cooperate with Nature you will want what is good for you and you will eat what is right for your body.

The following are some ideas of how to eat on a daily basis.

Green vegetables are rich in vitamin B, A, C, K and minerals. Some examples are kale, parsley, collards, and other mildly cooked greens. Vitamin B protects brain cells and mitochondria. Vitamin A and C improves immune cells. Vitamin K keeps bones and blood vessels healthy. Minerals are co-factors for hundreds of co-enzymes in the body. Daily greens lower the risk for cataracts and macular degeneration, a leading cause of blindness in the U.S.

Sulfur rich foods:

- Brain, kidneys and liver.
- The cabbage family - include arugula, bok choy, broccoli, broccoli sprouts, Brussels sprouts, cabbage, cauliflower, Swiss chard, collards, kale, kohlrabi, mustard greens, radishes, rutabaga, turnips, turnip greens and watercress.
- Onions, garlic, leeks, shallots, mushrooms and asparagus are high in sulfur.

Have three different color vegetables daily, which affect the retina, mitochondria, brain cells and toxin removal.

- Some examples are: beets, carrots, berries, peaches, oranges, peppers, and red cabbage, red wine, green tea, and apples.
- Colored vegetables have flavonoids, polyphenols, which supports retina, mitochondria and toxin removal.
    - o Mitochondria are sometimes described as "cellular power plants" because they generate most of the cell's supply of adenosine triphosphate (ATP), used as a source of chemical energy.
    - o Flavonoids have diverse beneficial biochemical and antioxidant effects.
    - o Polyphenol is a very high antioxidant.

Omega-3 fatty acids also known as polyunsaturated fatty acids (PUFAs) play a crucial role in brain function, as well as normal growth and development. They have also become popular because they may reduce the risk of heart disease. Omega-3 fatty acids can be found in fish, such as salmon, tuna, and halibut, other seafood including algae and krill, some plants, and nut oils.

Seaweed, which is high in iodine and selenium, should be eaten at least once per week. Helps the nerves (myelin), removes toxins and decreases cancer risk (breast and prostate are known ones).

Reducing grains (wheat, corn, rye and barley), potato, and dairy have been known to reduce the risk for food allergies and can allow you to increase vitamin and mineral content from your food intake.

Mindful Eating

I cannot end this chapter unless I have talked about the way you are eating your food and your mental attitude while eating. There is an old saying that says, "Chew your liquids and drink your solids." What this means to me is that we should chew our solid food until it liquefies before swallowing and chew our liquids to allow time for the amylase (enzyme in the mouth) to start the breaking down process of nutrients for digestion.

In the fast paced, sped up world we live in today, it is no wonder that many people have digestive disorders. There isn't much time in the day to sit down and enjoy our meals anymore. Observe others eating the next time you go out to dinner and you might be shocked at how some shovel down their food without any apparent consciousness. You might have even observed this with yourself, and may have felt the uncomfortable effects of gas and bloating after gobbling down food. Slowing down and chewing your food well with mindfulness will help improve your digestion. Every so often, as a reminder to myself to slow down and to connect with the food I am about to eat, I prepare and eat a meal in a ceremonial atmosphere. It is a semi-meditation or prayer mindset throughout the process. I give thanks and gratitude for the abundance that I have. I am grateful for the farmer that conscientiously grew and or raised the food, the delivery person that took it to market, the free-range hens for their eggs, and the ocean that provided the seaweed. I am thankful and grateful to the plants and animals. I am grateful for a healthy, functional and youthful, body, mind and spirit.

Practice a mindset when you arrive to the table to eat in which your business or domestic cares are left behind. Have meals with those who carry no distraction from the enjoyment of your meal. This way, you can develop a habit of giving your full, undivided attention to the act of eating while at the table. This you absolutely can do. Be cheerful at the table and take a moderate portion of the food. When you start to feel connected to your body and mind, select the food that attracts you the most, versus what you think will be good for you. Stay with what tastes good to you based on wisdom and sensitivity. It is wise to drop the idea of doing things because they are good for your health and do things because your body wants or needs them. Select the food you want the most and which resonates the most for your body. Be grateful and give thanks to *Kumukahi* that you have recognized the gifts that you were given to eat and digest in a *pono* way, and take a moderate mouthful at a time. Focus your attention on the taste of the food and not on the act of chewing. Don't be concerned with how long it takes to chew, or speculate as to what you want to eat next or anticipate the taste of the next thing. Don't worry if there is enough or if you will get your share. Think of the taste of what you have in your mouth. Another challenge to overcome is the anticipation of what dish will be next or what desert you will have after dinner.

Like in meditation, when you find your mind drifting off, focus back on the activity at hand. In meditation it is the breath, in eating it is the taste. Think of how good the food tastes and how your digestion and assimilation are doing a great job. It may take weeks or months, but in time you will experience a healthful pleasure you may not have known. If you want ideal health then it would be wise to think about these ways of eating. Through *no'ono'o pono* (determination, perseverance, discipline) you can and will keep your mind on the act of eating. When this is done correctly, digestion, assimilation, and the building of a healthy body will be the outcome.

I am thankful for the hands that planted this healthy
food, to the person that delivered it to the market,
and to the person that prepared this meal.

Notes

CHAPTER 12

Hiamoe Ola
Healthy Sleep

Rejuvenation and vitality is critical for ideal health and is renewed in quality through natural sleep. The indigenous Hawaiians in the past slept when the sun went down and woke either before or just as the sun rose. They kept in tune with the pulse of *Kumukahi* and Nature. All human beings, animals, insects, plants and other living things have a period of rest and recuperation. It is at this moment that we connect with the Principles of Life in nature so that our living self can be renewed. It is in sleep that our cells throughout our body are recharged with vitality and the Principles of Health within us is given new life. It is then vitally important that we sleep in a healthy and natural manner. For example, be sure you have fresh air circulating in your room versus stagnant or "dead" air no matter how cold or hot it may be outside. This is an important ingredient for healthy sleep. You are not sleeping in an ideal healthy way if the air is not naturally circulating throughout your bedroom from the outside.

Another ingredient for healthy sleep is your mental attitude prior to going to bed. My ancestors always cleared their mind through *ho'oponopono* before the setting sun each and every day of their lives. Never go to sleep angry or depressed; go there with joy and love. Before going to bed, give thanks and gratitude to *Kumukahi* for the abundance of health and joy.

My ancestors also created positive affirmations before actually falling asleep so a positive feeling would enter their REM sleep (rapid eye movement). This is the state of sleep that allows you to remember your dreams. Creating a positive mantra helps the subconscious mind to help manifest positive outcomes for your life. As an example, prior to sleeping and the moment I wake, I visualize repeatedly the phrase, "I am grateful, happy, healthy, financially and spiritually abundant."

Anatomy of sleep

The human body has an internal clock that regulates the cycle of sleep (*hiamoe*) and waking (*e ala*). This clock is located in the brain (suprachiasmatic nucleus) and has a connection to the cycles of the sun and moon. It is much more difficult and unhealthy to force your body and your body clock to do what you demand. Not only is it better the other way around, but also it is much healthier. Adapt or re-tune yourself to your body clock.

The indigenous people of the not-so-distant-past stayed in tune with Nature and the cycle of life because they didn't have the distractions that we have today. Late night activities like watching television, surfing the Internet, computer games and electricity that gives us light to keep us awake long after the sun has set.

Sleep deprivation is a common occurrence today and is the signal that we are forcing our body to be out of sync with our body clock. We are staying awake far beyond our physical limits. We have too many extracurricular activities; stress is at an all time high, more so in my lifetime than my parents; we have too much night light and electronics, and not enough time to slow down to take a breath.

A normal person has a body clock that resets itself in the morning with activity and sunlight. Thus a normal individual easily and naturally adjusts to the standard day-night cycle.

There are two main mechanisms that regulate sleepiness. One is the body clock and the other is the wake-regulator. Our body clock produces increased sleepiness every 24 hours (roughly). The wake-regulator increases drowsiness with prolonged wakefulness. For example, the longer we do not sleep, the sleepier we are. In scientific literature, these two mechanisms are called the circadian and homeostatic regulation of sleep. These components that control sleep are described below.

- Circadian clock: produces sleepiness in a 24-hour cycle.
- Homeostatic control: wake- regulator that measures the wake period and triggers sleepiness after we are awake for a while.

Better sleep habits

- Schedule your sleep patterns.
  - o o to bed and wake each day at the same time including weekends, holidays and days off. Consistency reinforces your body's sleep-wake cycle. If at times you don't fall asleep at your scheduled sleep time within 30 minutes, get up and do something relaxing. Return to bed when you are tired. Fighting to go to sleep may engender the opposite result.
- Watch what you eat and drink.
  - o Don't go to bed either hungry, or stuffed, as either may keep you up. Give yourself at least one hour after eating before your bedtime. Limit how much you drink before sleeping to prevent bathroom runs in the middle of the night.
- Have an evening ritual.
  - o Give your body a 'heads up' to wind down. For example, an herbal bath, warm shower, or reading a book you have been waiting to read, but didn't have the time with lights dimmed low. These kinds of activities encourage a positive transition between waking state and sleeping state. Turn off all electronics at least 30 minutes before your scheduled bedtime, as this may inhibit your sleep patterns.
- A comfortable bed.
  - o Create a room that's ideal for sleeping. Have a comfortable mattress and appropriate and comfortable bedding for that time of year. If your partner snores, arrange for separate

sleeping quarters. Pets and children can also interfere with your sleep patterns.

- Exercise
    o Light workouts on a regular basis, but obviously not before bedtime.
- Things to avoid.
    o Alcohol, caffeine, heavy, spicy or sugary foods at least a few hours before bedtime.
- Meditation (See chapter 14).
    o Techniques that calm the mind like meditation and/or deep breathing exercises.

Through repetition and diligence, you may find that the ingredients for a healthy sleep are not difficult. Have clean circulating air from the outdoors while you sleep and do a few minutes of mind calming techniques like meditation prior to going to bed. Clearing the mind of the day's activities prior to sleeping also helps the sleep to be deep and productive. Observe these guidelines and go to bed in a grateful, thankful, and positive frame of mind, and you will reap the benefits.

If you have moments of difficulty falling asleep, do not worry or give it much thought. While you lie awake, focus on your positive mantra and form your conception of health. Meditate with thankfulness on the abundant life that you have. Observe your natural breathing rhythm and trust and know (*ho'ona'au pono*) that you will sleep in due time.

Through practice and diligence, the cultivation of ideal health can be easy, simple, natural, and joyful. You only have to eliminate artificial thought of any kind and eat, drink, breathe, and sleep in the most natural and *pono* way while thinking of only health. The outcome will undoubtedly result in being well.

If I have harmed or wronged anyone today knowingly or unknowingly, I release this energy and replace it with love.

Notes

CHAPTER 13

Ho'oma'ema'e
Fasting/Cleansing

Fasting and cleansing have been used for thousands of years in Polynesia as a natural healing therapy to awaken the body's own healing mechanisms, the Principle of Health within. Where modern medicine attempts to alleviate outer symptoms of a health condition, fasting and cleansing affects healing from the inside out. When properly utilized, fasting and cleansing (SUPERVISED is recommended if haven't done it before) are a safe and effective means of maximizing the body's self-healing capacities.

Although fasting and cleansing are technically two different detoxification processes, this chapter will be focusing primarily on fasting as a detoxifying system. Intentional fasting is the complete abstinence from all food substances except pure water, in an environment of total rest. Cleansing varies depending on its approach and intention in assisting the body to detoxify and rebuild itself. For example, a juice fast, which is really a cleanse, involves drinking only specific juiced vegetables and fruits that have been prepared with a blender or an auger system juicer. Eating specific foods that are known to be good for cleansing the body is also considered cleansing. For example, watermelon is a great cleanser and so is grape juice. Indigenous Botanicals' 60-day Hawaiian Cleansing and Detoxification program, which involves taking herbal formulations with a periodic salt water flush, and eating pure healthy foods is a cleanse. However, our 4-day fasting program, which uses the same ingredients as the 60-day program, but taken more aggressively using diluted grape juice and herbs with no food can be considered a fast. The outcome of both varies tremendously. The 4-day program gets faster results and the 60-day program takes a little longer for a similar outcome, but is great for those that cannot fast or may have a hard time disciplining themselves.

> *"Everyone has a doctor in him; we just have to help him in his work. The natural healing force within each one of us is the greatest force in getting well…to eat when you are sick, is to feed your sickness."*
>
> - Hippocrates, one of the three
> fathers of Western medicine

So you may be thinking, why do I need to fast and how do fasting affect my health and longevity? Keep in mind that fasting is only one part of the total health picture. Health and vitality results from living healthful each and everyday of your life. No matter how successful a fasting experience might be, it needs to be followed by a consistently healthy lifestyle. The requirements of health must continue to be provided - especially in the areas of diet, environment, activity and psychology.

During the past thirty plus years I've worked with thousands of patients from all over the world who have had a wide variety of disorders and health concerns. Many of these patients required some period of supervised fasting to achieve their immediate and long-term health goals. Virtually all of them needed to make lifestyle changes to achieve improved health. Fasting made the transition easier.

My observation is that the best motivating factor in helping people adopt healthful living practices is often the positive reinforcement that comes with feeling good and healthy. Supervised fasting, for as few as two to four days, will often dramatically accomplish this. It can shorten the time it takes for an individual to make the transition from a conventional diet and lifestyle (with all the associated addictions, pains, fatigue and disease) to the independent and energetic state associated with healthful living. Indigenous Botanicals' 60-Day Cleansing program is also an excellent way of finding that positive reinforcement of transitioning to a more healthful lifestyle.

In the early days with Auntie Margaret in Kona, HI, during many of our fasting programs, it was the positive physical and emotional results that helped people transition quicker to a healthier lifestyle change. In those days we would inspect what people were eliminating, which required each person standing next to his or her "bucket of truth." Auntie Margaret would then show each person what he or she was eliminating and why they were having the symptoms they came in with.

Through the use of iridology technology, I would correlate Auntie Margaret's assessment of the small and large intestines from the elimination bucket with my findings. Iridology is the study of the color, pigmentations, and structure of the iris of the eye as they relate genetically through reflex response to the strengths and deficiencies of the body systems. It is one of the best assessment tools available to be able to know the areas of the body that are genetically strong as well as deficient. I've been using and studying iridology for over thirty years and it never ceases to amaze me.

Seeing what people were eliminating and correlating it with my iridology findings was a huge learning curve for me especially with Auntie Margaret's input. In the evenings after "bucket inspections," we would compare notes and verify specific lifestyle changes ideal for each individual's needs. For example, if I saw a weakness in the walls of a specific segment of the large intestines through iridology, Auntie Margaret would point it out in the 'pan of elimination.' This weakening of the walls is commonly referred to as "ballooning." This is when part of the colon has been over stretched for a long period of time and some of its elasticity has been lost, which leads to diminish peristaltic action. Ballooning almost always correlates to constipation and stagnation. Our discussion led to the use of alfalfa tablets or capsules to assist in the toning of the ballooning intestines, which would assist in bringing function back to that organ. Specific dietary changes were also discussed to further help this particular individual in his path to having a strong, healthy, functional body, mind and soul. We found iridology and "bucket inspections," to be the fastest, safest, cheapest way of evaluating a person's digestive and other organ systems and to prescribe a specific course of action.

Once, through iridology, I observed a number of diverticula located in the mid-descending colon of a particular patient. Diverticula are out-pouching (pouches) of the walls of the large intestine. If these pouches develop inflammation or infection, it is called diverticulitis. Diverticulitis happens when waste matter or feces gets trapped in the pouches, which allows bacteria to grow, that leads to inflammation or infection. The cause is unknown, but it is usually due to poor dietary lifestyle habits especially eating on the run and not drinking enough water. This particular middle-aged male patient had been a vegetarian for the last seven years so typically there wouldn't be any cause for concern. When Auntie Margaret inspected the physical pouches, however, a story unfolded. After careful dissection of the eliminated specimen (the herbal formulation in the fast draws out a casing from the small and large intestine made of old waste matter), we found hamburger in one of the pouches. So he had undigested food lodged in one of the pouches that had been sitting there for years. We further determined that that part of the large intestine correlated to the kidneys and adrenal glands that had given him discomfort. As soon as the fast was over, his symptoms disappeared.

When there is old waste material embedded in the large intestine it causes what is called "autointoxication." This self-poisoning results from the absorption of waste products of metabolism, decomposed intestinal matter, or other toxins produced within the body. Although this person was a vegetarian for seven years, seeing the results from his fast further encouraged him to stay on track and to continue to do periodic cleansing. He felt great and expressed a renewed sense of vitality. Those around him in the program didn't need any more convincing to be on their path of maintaining a healthy dietary lifestyle habit and to do periodic cleansing.

I have compiled a short list of reasons why you may want to consider doing colon cleanses.

- Lifestyle – Poor dietary habits can lead to weakness in the digestive system, which leads to health compromises, disease and degeneration.
- Air pollution – Increase free radicals from man-made pollutants leading to all kinds of health compromises.
- Water pollution – Our water supply is in constant need of being treated due to pollutants getting into the water table. One startling finding is the amount of medication, hormone therapy, etc. being flushed down the toilet through urination and contaminating the water source of that community.
- Food pollution – We consume genetically modified foods, which our bodies cannot recognize or digest. Much of our foods today are sprayed with pesticides and the soil is saturated with chemical fertilizers. We also tend to over-cook our food and kill the nutritional enzymes necessary for digestion.
- Autointoxication – As described above, it ultimately leads to degeneration of our body tissues.
- Pancreatic deficiencies – From the overconsumption of processed sugar especially fructose.
- Heavy metals and Mercury – When they get lodged in the colon it can interfere with cell communication. In my days you could find a lot of mercury in dental work, but I believe that has improved over the years.
- Congested liver – When the liver is compromised it is more difficult to convert food into a form that the body can use. Diet, overuse of alcohol, drugs, and compromise organs of elimination (colon, skin, kidneys and lungs) create problems with the liver.
- Unwanted pathogens – Parasites and bad bacteria.
- Poor digestion – Weakness in the stomach's ability to digest food properly and entirely diminishes the body's ability to absorb quality nutrition for proper assimilation.

The colon consists of four sections: the ascending colon, the transverse colon, the descending colon, and the sigmoid colon. The colon is the last part of the digestive system and its function is to extract water and salt from solid wastes before they are eliminated from the body. The gut flora (largely bacterial – most of which are good) helps the fermentation of unabsorbed materials. Maintaining a clean colon is the foundation to wellness.

Below are a few symptoms that I have had success with using fasting, ho'opono, herbs, and nutritional intervention.

- Constipation, diarrhea, sluggish elimination, irregular bowel movements.
- Frequent headaches with no apparent cause.
- Skin problems, rashes, boils, pimples, and acne.
- Frequent congestion, colds, and viruses.
- General aches and pains that migrate from one place to another.
- Low back pain.
- Lowered resistance to infections.
- Low energy, loss of vitality for no apparent cause.
- Needing to sleep longer at night.
- Flatulence and frequent stomach disorders.
- Bad breath and foul smelling stool.
- Allergies, intolerance to certain foods, especially fatty ones.
- Premenstrual syndrome, breast soreness, vaginal infections.
- Fibromyalgia/chronic fatigue.
- Depression (especially manic).
- Addictions.
    - Addictions to drugs such as alcohol, cocaine, nicotine and caffeine are examples where fasting can dramatically reduce the often long-drawn-out withdrawal symptoms that prevent many people from becoming drug-free. Most people are surprised at how easy it is to quit smoking or drinking with the help of fasting.

Here is another reason why you may want to consider periodic fasting. Colorectal cancer is the third most common cancer diagnosed in both men and women in the United States. The American Cancer Society's most recent estimates for the number of colorectal cancer cases in the United States for 2012 are:

- 103,170 new cases of colon cancer
- 40,290 new cases of rectal cancer

Overall, the lifetime risk of developing colorectal cancer is about 1 in 20 (5.1%). This risk is slightly lower in women than in men. Colorectal cancer is the third leading cause of cancer-related deaths in the United States when men and women are considered separately, and the second leading cause when both sexes are combined. It is expected to cause about 51,690 deaths during 2012.

It should be noted that the National Cancer Institute's (NCI) investment in colorectal cancer research increased from $244.1 million in fiscal year (FY) 2006 to $270.4 million in FY 2010. In addition, NCI supported $58.6 million in colorectal cancer research in FY 2009 and 2010 using funding from the American Recovery and Reinvestment Act (ARRA). Yet, they are no closer to finding solutions for recovery than they were ten years ago. Further more, there has not been any substantial research into fasting and nutritional programs as a possible solution when clinical and field evidence show overwhelming positive results.

Another common problem I see often is Irritable Bowel Syndrome (IBS), which affects over 40 million people in the U.S. with symptoms of diarrhea, constipation, gas, and bloating. IBS can be triggered by a number of factors, including stress, hormonal changes associated with menopause, and even the disruption of the brain neurotransmitter serotonin that helps regulate the digestive system.

In my professional opinion, on-going colon cleansing and dietary adjustment is often the only treatment necessary to relieve IBS. Taking a teaspoon of an appropriate colon cleansing formula on a daily basis in the morning and evening will definitely help to relieve symptoms and keep things flowing. With the recent research showing fructose as a possible trigger for IBS, it would be wise to completely eliminate this from your diet as well. Fructose was once embraced as an alternative to sugar, but the evidence is showing that by restricting this fake sugar, IBS can be reduced. So read the labels!

If your body is unable to absorb fructose during digestion, the fructose passes into the colon where it's consumed by bacteria. When bacteria digests fructose in the colon, acids and gases are produced that trigger IBS symptoms such as bloating, cramping and diarrhea. Some of the gases pass into the bloodstream, and can then be detected in the breath, which is why the breath test is an effective way to diagnose fructose intolerance.

Periodic fasting or cleansing can optimize digestion, which can prevent deficiencies that the average person experiences. For example, it is estimated that at least 50% of Americans are deficient in vitamin D, iodine, and B12. Taking supplementation to counter these deficiencies are often ineffective due to poor fire in the digestive system and poor absorption abilities.

Current research has linked vitamin D deficiency (below optimized levels) with at least 17 varieties of cancer as well as: heart disease, stroke, high blood pressure, autoimmune diseases like multiple sclerosis, diabetes, depression, obesity, chronic muscle and/or joint pain, muscle weakness, muscle wasting, osteoarthritis, osteoporosis, birth defects, periodontal disease, and more. One obvious reason for vitamin D deficiency is the fact that we spend more time indoors than outdoors and when we are outdoors we use sunscreen to block out important UVB rays. UVB rays are only available when the UV index is above 3. Personally, I don't recommend using sunscreen, but rather integrating or transitioning your time in the sun with appropriate natural protection such as fresh, raw aloe vera applied topically. Raw, extra virgin coconut oil, is also great to use after your time in the sun, something Hawaiians did successfully for generations.

Vitamin B12 improves mood, energy and focus. It improves sleep, appetite, motivation, movement, and cognition. It protects us from heart attacks, strokes and arterial plaque. It repairs and supports the nervous system while maintaining brain chemistry and synthesizing neurotransmitters like dopamine, serotonin and epinephrine.

Iodine fights and prevents infections, protects against toxins and heavy metals, supports thyroid and hormones, improves memory, mood and energy, prevents goiter and helps prevent cancer. Symptoms of deficiency can be fatigue, cold hands and feet, foggy thinking, increased need for sleep, dry skin, weight gain and constipation.

Cleansing will help balance blood sugar levels to help the body detoxify optimally. Cleansing can heal the intestinal villi, which improves absorption of nutrients and the removal of waste. It can de-stagnate the lymphatic system, which drains the gut through the GALT (Gut Associated Lymphatic Tissue) where 80% of the body's immune system is housed. It thins the bile, which allows for adequate bile flow that is important for the detoxification channels of the body. It flushes the liver for optimal function that can improve metabolizing toxic chemicals stored in fat cells. Cleansing regulates stomach acid to properly break down and assimilate food.

Purging the digestive tract eliminates the source of toxicity or poisoning. This process allows regeneration of the blood and energy naturally. Cleansing the colon will enhance the body's ability to repair itself.

Many people say that they want to lose the fat from around their waistline, which they call their stomach. Unfortunately, they are not aware that this is not their stomach and the protruding section is probably not fat either. The odds are that it's an obstructed colon congested with stagnate waste and toxins bulging outwards.

Your stomach lies just below the front rib cage. It's not centered, but a bit off to the left. This part of your body doesn't bulge much. The colon is right behind the waistline. This is the area where some people have the most weight. Anyone who is sick has elimination trouble, whether they know it or not. If you do not get your bowels back to functioning properly, all other therapies, treatments, supplements or other holistic intervention diminishes a positive outcome. Proper bowel function is an essential prerequisite for staying healthy, and overcoming sickness and disease.

An unhealthy colon is the seat of most illness. Colds, flu, cancer, cardiovascular disease, arthritis, and allergies are all examples of diseases caused by excessive amounts of poor-quality food combined with poor elimination. When you don't eliminate properly, food may stay in the colon for days, weeks, months, even years, putrefying and then poisoning your entire system. In most cases, the level of any disease is directly proportional to the level of toxicity in the body.

The digestive system's primary function is to convert food into energy and convert waste into excretal material. It is also responsible for the absorption and digestion of all digestible products. The digestive system sustains life via its ability to break down food into molecules to provide nutrients for its systems, tissue, and bodily fluids. Without the digestive system, all other systems would eventually fail to operate, fluids would either stop production or dry up, and tissue would deteriorate.

Digestible food is utilized at the cellular level, of which the digestive system is in charge. Nutrients from food are broken down and the remaining nutrients are used for chemical reactions. These reactions allow cells throughout the body to reproduce, repair themselves, and maintain cellular division. Fasting and cleansing also generates cellular growth, heat production, energy production, and the synthesis of enzymes, which allow these functions to occur.

Food cannot be used at a cellular level until it has been properly broken down both mechanically and chemically. The broken down and digested foods turn into nutrients which are then absorbed through the intestinal wall. The nutrients are then transferred to the cells via the blood stream and delivered to the site of cells, which are in need of the nutrients. Food is considered digested only after absorption, which applies to a small percentage of food as most of the food eaten is never absorbed and is passed through the excretory system with its nutrients unabsorbed. Only usable nutrients and chemicals are absorbed and brought to the appropriate cellular group for nutritional function. It is therefore critical that we are able to maximize our ability to accomplish all these acts.

The Basic Process of Digestion

1.   Ingestion is the process of eating. In reference to the digestive system, this typically means food, however it may include vitamin supplements, medications, and liquids.

2.   Mastication is the process of mixing edible elements with saliva for the purposes of breaking the edible elements down. This process typically involves chewing. There is an old saying, "Drink your solids and eat your liquids." Proper digestion starts in the mouth. The more saliva is involved the better the digestion of nutrients.

3.   Deglutition refers to the process of moving edible elements from the mouth down through the esophagus and into the stomach. Digestion is the process of breaking down the edible elements and preparing them for absorption through the intestinal wall and used by the cells.

4.   Absorption refers to the process of passing the broken down edible elements through the intestinal wall into the blood stream where either blood cells or lymph cells retrieve the nutrients and carry them off toward their destination.

5.   Peristalsis is the action of processing waste by the intestinal tract, which resembles wave-like motions to help pass the solid waste through the intestines.

6. Defecation is the final process in the digestive system, which removes solid waste product in the form of fecal matter from the body.

The digestive system is generally divided into specific functional and anatomical groups that consist of the digestive tract, the tubular gastrointestinal tract, and the accessory digestive organs. The tubular gastrointestinal tract is one continuous tract, shaped for the most part as a cylinder that runs from the mouth to the anus creating a pathway for food, nutrients, and waste. At 30 feet long, it traverses the thoracic cavity and enters the abdominal cavity along the diaphragm and includes the oral cavity, thorax, esophagus, stomach, small intestines, and large intestines. The accessory digestive organs, those that are vital to the process but cannot otherwise be classified, include the teeth, tongue, liver, salivary glands, pancreas, and gallbladder.

It takes about 24 to 48 hours for food to travel through the entire digestive tract depending on the type of food eaten. The breakdown of edible food and therefore the breakdown of molecules with vital value to the body's cells, is done in the body's own version of an assembly line. Nutritional value is removed from the food on a molecular level and brought to the body's cells for nutritional absorption.

When properly applied and conducted, therapeutic fasting is one of the most potent tools available for assisting the body in healing itself. When abused or applied unwisely, harm can result. The most important advice I can give anyone regarding fasting is this.

*If you are going to undertake a fast, do
it right or don't do it at all!*

The most obvious indication for therapeutic fasting is the lack of appetite that may be associated with a mild to acute disease. When the body generates a healing crisis in acute disease, it is generally best to eliminate the intake of food until the crisis has resolved and hunger returns. That might mean skipping a meal or two or even skipping many meals. Theses acute symptoms include things like fever, inflammation, pain, etc. It is in acute disease that I see the most dramatic results from short term fasting.

Fasting is also effectively utilized in chronic disease. Chronic disease often has its origin in acute diseases that never resolved or were suppressed. Fasting allows the body an opportunity to generate an acute response in a chronic condition. It is in the fasting state that the body is given the opportunity to purify its tissues, to eliminate undesirable tissue accumulations, growth, etc. It also allows the body an opportunity to let stressed and abused tissues heal.

The scientific and medical literature contains literally hundreds of papers dealing with the therapeutic use of fasting. Again, it has been extensively used in the treatment of a variety of conditions, including obesity, diabetes, epilepsy, atherosclerotic vascular disease, congestive heart failure, cancer, autoimmune disease such as rheumatoid arthritis, psychiatric disorders including schizophrenia, and as a desensitization tool in the treatment of hypersensitivity and allergies.

Fasting provides an opportunity for the organism to "clean house," physically and mentally; for accumulated debris to be eliminated; and to allow for the introspection that is so often lacking in the rush of modern day life.

There are individuals who are not good candidates for therapeutic fasting and there are also a few conditions that are contraindicated. The greatest contraindication to fasting is fear. A lack of understanding of the fasting process can present overwhelming problems. Extreme weakness in various diseases associated with muscular wasting may also contraindicate fasting. There are numerous medications that can complicate the fasting process. Inadequate nutrient reserves would be another potential contraindication to fasting as it takes energy to fast. Certain types of cancer and severe kidney disease may also make an individual a poor fasting candidate.

With proper supervision and careful clinical monitoring, therapeutic fasting is safe and effective as a means of helping the body heal itself. But as with any activity there are inherent risks. I advise anyone contemplating a therapeutic fast to consider utilizing a professional who is trained in its use.

Whatever the indication for therapeutic fasting, it is essential that the individual be placed in an environment conducive to complete rest, like a retreat center. The body needs to adjust to the fasting physiology so the importance of rest should not be underestimated. Unnecessary demand for nutrient reserves must be avoided. It is not only the physical activity that needs to stop, but mental activity as well. That is why I highly recommend meditation during fasting.

In some cases, a pre-fasting evaluation should be completed before therapeutic fasting is considered, especially in extreme cases. This means taking a complete health history, including an evaluation of previous illnesses, injury and treatment. An assessment is made of the current symptoms and current treatment being undertaken. A family history is also of interest. Next, a comprehensive physical exam should be performed. Appropriate laboratory procedures such as the utilization of urinalysis or blood evaluations should also be performed as well. These procedures provide the practitioner with the information needed to determine if therapeutic fasting is indicated as well as providing a base line that can be used to establish each individual person's normal bio-physiological findings. Without a good base line, it can be very difficult to differentiate a positive healing crisis from a physiological compromise. For example, a person who develops a skin rash on the fifth day of a fast might be treated very differently from an individual who starts the fast with the same condition.

Although an experienced practitioner can estimate the length of a fast needed, none of us have crystal balls. Its important to go into the fast with a willingness to allow the body to tell us what is indicated. The idea is to fast as briefly as possible, but as long as necessary to allow the body to generate and resolve any possible healing crises that might result.

The physiology of fasting has been extensively studied and three phases of fasting have been identified. The first phase can be called the gastrointestinal phase. It consists of approximately the first six hours after the last meal. During this phase the body uses glucose, amino acids and fats, as they are absorbed from the intestinal tract. Phase two lasts for more or less the next two days. During this time the body will use its glycogen (sugar) reserves that are stored in the muscle and liver cells. These glycogen reserves are mobilized to provide the central nervous system, including the brain, with its normal fuel, glucose. Within a few hours the body begins to convert adipose (fat) tissue into fatty acids. Were it not for the body's ability to switch fuels and enter phase three, where the body switches from glucose to fat metabolism, therapeutic fasting could not take place. The body's protein reserves would be quickly depleted.

Fortunately, this is not a problem. In fact, within ten hours from the last meal approximately 50% of muscle fuel is coming from fat. Even the brain itself begins to shift over the fat metabolism. As you can see, excess activity including excess emotional stress could increase the body's fuel needs, interfering with the optimum adaptation to the fasting state. Body reserves differ from individual to individual. But a "typical" 155-pound male at normal weight has enough reserves to fast for between two to four months. If the fast were allowed to continue beyond the individual's reserves, starvation would ensue and serious damage and eventually death would occur.

As with all aspects of fasting, proper termination of the fast is a highly individual matter. The decision to terminate a fast is based on an evaluation of numerous factors, including the patient's history, symptomatic presentation, examination results, laboratory results, as well as their psychological state and personal circumstances.

One of the characteristics of therapeutic fasting is the "healing crisis." A healing crisis may occur when the vital forces within the body build up enough strength to handle detoxification. When improvement occurs, vitality is restored to the body, and its self-healing mechanisms are awakened. As healing begins, symptoms reappear as part of the body's process of eliminating diseased cells and toxins from its tissues. It is important to understand the healing crisis and avoid interfering with this necessary and productive process. We always try to terminate a fast during a period of stability. Most fasts will be terminated with fresh fruits or vegetables or their juices.

> *"The witch doctor succeeds for the same reason all the rest of us succeed. Each patient carries his own doctor inside himself or herself. They come to us not knowing that cure. We are at our best when we give the doctor who resides within each patient a chance to go to work."*
> Albert Schweitzer, M.D.

The most important period of the fast is the initial re-introduction to eating. Returning to food intake too rapidly can spell disaster. Materials that have been mobilized during the fast must be eliminated. Improper eating or activity after the fast can seriously disrupt this process.

It is during the re-eating program that good dietary and lifestyle habits are reinforced. The body must be given an opportunity to develop a reference for whole, natural foods, appropriate physical activity, etc. No matter how successful your body is at resolving problems with a fasting process, long term dietary and life-style compliance will be necessary.

Fasting is not a cure. It is a process that facilitates the body's healing mechanisms. It is up to each individual to ensure that the requirements of health are provided on a continuing basis.

Therapeutic fasting means taking pure water while ensuring complete physical and emotional rest. This unique process maximizes the healing potential of the body, allowing it to "clean house" and quickly restore a state of higher health.

Therapeutic fasting should be supervised by a properly trained professional and should be followed by appropriate dietary and lifestyle modifications. When properly implemented, therapeutic fasting is extremely effective in creating an internal environment in which the body can do what it does best - heal it.

I let go of those things that do not serve my highest
good and I welcome ease and joy.

For those who want more detailed information on speeding up the process of establishing a strong foundation of being well, I recommend the 60-Day Hawaiian Cleanse & Detoxification Program or the Four Day Fasting Program, which is available through Indigenous Botanicals.

(www.indigenousbotanicals.net)

Notes

CHAPTER 14

Ho'okuano'o
Meditation

"As one travels over the world and observes the appalling conditions of poverty and the ugliness of man's relationship to man, it becomes obvious that there must be a total revolution. A different kind of culture must come into being. The old culture is almost dead and yet we are clinging to it. Those who are young revolt against it, but unfortunately have not found a way or a means, of transforming the essential quality of the human being, which is the mind. Unless there is a deep psychological revolution, mere reformation of the periphery will have little effect. This psychological revolution - which I think is the only revolution - is possible through meditation."

J. Krishnamurti 1976

Many Hawaiians today have long held the belief that the information passed down from their parents and grandparents about their cultural heritage and practices are family secrets and should remain so. I think this is a mistake. If you don't practice and share the healing work, especially the meditation practices, you lose it. A case in point, it's rare to find Hawaiians meditating at all these days. Originally, many *na kahuna*, or Hawaiian masters, understood that it was their *kuleana*, or responsibility, to celebrate aspects of their culture and history by sharing it with others. Meditation is part of life and part of the ancient Hawaiian heritage, not something foreign.

For generations, Hawaiians have been using meditation for everything, from planting and working with the weather, to fishing and athletic performances. There are endless forms of Hawaiian meditation; most of which are designed for specific purposes. In the case of being well, meditation can bring balance and alignment to our thoughts, words and actions. It is important to mention that meditation has very little meaning or value if you are not practicing it in a *pono* way. That is to say, eliminate fear, doubt, anger, greed and hate through *ho'oponopono* to get the most out of the practice of meditation.

Ho'okuano'o is the indigenous Hawaiian way of reuniting the soul with the higher consciousness, with *Kumukahi*. The soul manifests its consciousness and *mana* (life force) through the *'piko'* (chakra) or centers of light, or energy centers within the human cerebrospinal axis. It is within this bodily prism that the soul consciousness and life force become identified with physical limitations.

Our body is programmable by language, tones, words, symbols and thoughts, all of which carry a frequency. The kind of frequency created determines the focused outcome of the producer. Each individual must work on the inner process and development, in order to establish a conscious communication with their DNA, which is our superconductor that store light, therefore, information. When a large number of people collectively come together with higher intentions such as meditating on peace, violent potentials will dissolve. It is through meditation that all questions, all troubles, and all difficulties can be resolved or answered.

Certain tools can be used to enhance meditation and lend to their success. Meditation tools are like having a doctor's bag (metaphorically speaking); he or she never knows what they're going to use until the appropriate situation arises, but they have the knowledge of how to use the tools. Depending on the specific situation presented, the doctor's bag can range from fasting and cleansing, to movement exercises like *hula* and *lua* (a type of Hawaiian martial art), mind-body connection tools like herbs, teas, foods, sweats, and massage (i.e *Mana Lomi*®).

111

Meditation shouldn't be confused with everyday concentration. Concentration is focusing the mind with intent and determination on any line of thought. Meditation is the application of concentration solely to know *Kumukahi* or Cosmic Consciousness. The objective is to calm the mind and reach a high level of concentration on *Kumukahi. Ho'okuano'o* then is that specific form of concentration that is applied solely for the conscious connection of tuning in with Cosmic Consciousness, which is the Source of cosmic supply. The proficient student of this form of meditation not only achieves the power of attention and what it can accomplish, but also develops the power to control his or her destiny and prevent failure and disease. Through dedicated, persistent practice, you can learn how to revitalize and strengthen your own super-consciousness.

The specific meditation techniques described in this chapter can help pry open the lid of consciousness and release the foundation of joy from *Kumukahi*. It is this joy that will guide you to the right action in everything that serves your highest good. Once you experience the joy of *Kumukahi*, achieving most anything else will diminish in comparison. Your consciousness will expand. Nothing in this world will be able to persuade you to let go of this blissful state of consciousness that you will find in meditation. Meditation is the conscious relaxation of the mind from restlessness, which is the ideal way to know *Kumukahi*.

Frequent meditation practice changes your whole body and mind because by being in contact with *Kumukahi*, all things become harmonious; all things become one ocean of peace. In order to achieve full consciousness of this Supreme force, it is important to practice meditation consistently and seriously. Don't procrastinate. Don't put meditation off till tomorrow, for tomorrow may never come. Beginning meditation today will generate more motivation to meditate more deeply tomorrow. Don't let bad habits or vanity engagements persuade you away from contacting *Kumukahi*.

Meditation is about reconnecting with your soul. It is a practice that allows you to disconnect from your physical body and remember that you are a soul. When you begin to relate yourself to the soul, you become more aware of your past experiences. You will know that you have originated from *Kumukahi*.

In your inner contact with *Kumukahi* you will find the memory and experiences of all your lives. Your consciousness will reawaken. Meditation can lead you to remember that you are not mortal, but that you are one with *Kumukahi*. When not meditating you remember you are mortal, but in meditation the opposite is true. Meditation means letting go of the consciousness of the physical body, remembering who you really are, and then coming back out of meditation and being more able to control your physical body. When the mind is always thinking about the body it becomes limited by it. When the mind constantly meditates on the Infinite it becomes unlimited. Meditation is the art of transferring the attention from finite things to the Infinite. Meditation means constantly thinking of the unlimited space inside and outside, so that the soul can let go of its attachments to the limited physical body. Letting go of limitations leads us to remembering our cosmic self as part of *Kumukahi*. Think of it in terms of *Kumukahi* being the Spirit Ocean and your soul as the wave of that ocean. The Spirit Ocean knows that it has many soul waves, but each soul wave needs to remember, by meditation, that it is the Spirit Ocean. Each little soul wave must let go of its perception that it is infinitely small, and separate from the whole. Instead, concentrate on the vast universe as its own big body of which the physical body is just a tiny part.

Knowing *Kumukahi* through meditation will reveal to you that this life is only a dream. You will realize that life is only a drama in a movie, and that you are eternal, that you were never sick, that you were never dead, and you were never unhappy. Meditation can enable you to contact the super consciousness of the soul and through that the cosmic consciousness of *Kumukahi* (Spirit), giving you everlasting peace, harmony, and the tranquility of mind inherent in our true selves.

Some known benefits from meditation:

Lowers oxygen consumption and respiratory rate, increases blood flow and lowers heart rate, increases exercise endurance, improves physical relaxation, normalizes blood pressure, reduces anxiety attacks, reduces PMS symptoms, enhances immune system, helps post-operative healing, lowers risk for cardiovascular disease, slows aging process, improves brain function, improves breathing disorders, relaxes nervous system, builds self-confidence, improves mood and behavior, helps focus and concentration efforts, improves learning ability and memory, increases vitality and rejuvenation, improves intuition, increases productivity, improves relationships with others, strengthens will power, improves communication between the brain's two hemispheres, lessens tendency to worry, provides peace of mind and happiness, helps you discover your purpose, increases self-awareness, increases compassion, grows wisdom, brings harmony to body, mind and soul, creates a deeper relationship with *Kumukahi*, helps living in the present moment, and deepens the capacity to love.

There are many meditation techniques that I use that have helped a lot of people in their everyday lives. For the purpose of this book, however, I would like to share just five of them. Each technique prepares the meditating person to go deeper into a state of stillness and eventually to experience breathless states. The first, *Alo-Ha*, is to focus the attention and to calm the mind through the observation of the breath. The second, *Kukulu 'O Ke Ao*, is about protection and bringing harmony into the surrounding area and the self. The third, *Mamao Aku Ola*, is for distant healing. The fourth, *Ha 'Ehiku*, focuses on intentions and positive outcomes. The fifth, *Ka Leo 'O Ke Kai*, is about focusing our attention to the harmonious astral sounds produced by our energy (chakra) centers.

When and Where to Meditate

If possible, find a nice little quiet place to be used only for meditation. This will assist in achieving ideal divine, silence consciousness. Any quiet room that is neither too warm nor too cold, or a forest in the summer, or a shoreline in the pacific... any one of these is suitable for meditation. Riding on an airplane, or train, or boat, you can still practice meditation while pretending to be asleep.

Ideally, but not necessarily, place a *lauhala* mat or facsimile on your chair or ground that you will be sitting on to insulate your body against the Earth's opposite magnetic pull. This opposite magnetism can impede the *mana* (life currents) and *'ike* (consciousness) flow, which you are trying to draw upward through the spinal centers to the higher centers of divine consciousness in the brain.

Practice meditation in the early morning and before going to sleep at night. In the evenings give yourself at least an hour after a meal before meditating. For the beginner, it is best to start with about fifteen minute meditations each time then build to about thirty minutes or more morning and night. The longer you practice with intensity the greater your spiritual advancement, which is the joyful contact to *Kumukahi*. Breathless state of consciousness brings longevity and what the ancient Hawaiians called *make 'ole* (deathlessness). Breath is the cord, which ties the soul to the body. Master it and you will be free.

The five meditations

- Alo – Ha
- Kukulu 'o ke ao
- Mamao aku ola
- Ha 'ehiku
- Ka leo 'o ke kai

ALO-HA

The *Alo-Ha* meditation technique is a good basic technique and helps the person meditating to bring his or her attention into focus. When we're born, we're very connected to our soul and to our physical selves. As we get older and into our way of living we often, due to our life's circumstances, become "separated." Therefore, this meditation can help reunite our body and our soul. This technique has two components -- "*Alo*," which literally means, "being in the presence of" or "connected, as one," and "*Ha*," which means "the essence of life from where the evolutionary process unfolds." "*Alo*" also is the vibration of the inhale breath and "*Ha*" the vibration of the exhale breath. "*Alo*" and "*Ha*" calms the breath quickly, as it carries its astral vibration. Meditation is about focus, focus, focus and the *Alo-Ha* meditation brings the person's attention back into focus.

Alo- Hā can be performed anywhere, while running, hiking, walking, sitting or standing. The practitioner should naturally inhale on the *Alo* and exhale on the *Hā*. Observe yourself, observe your breath. Feel every muscle that moves from the natural movement of the breath.

Before starting *Alo-Ha*, practice the following breathing exercises seven to ten times:

- Inhale to a count of 7
- Hold the breath to a count of 7
- Exhale to a count of 7

If a 7 count is too long for you, then inhale, hold, and exhale the breath to a shorter count. Whatever number you decide to use, it should be the same for inhalation, hold, and exhalation.

With eyelids closed, or half closed, focus your eyes or attention at the point between the eyebrows. Inhale and exhale three times quickly then wait for the breath to start up again naturally. Observe each natural inhalation as it flows in and mentally chant "*Alo*" for the duration of that inhalation. Regardless if the inhalation is short or long or quick or slow, mentally continue the chant "*Alo*" without making a sound or movement of the tongue. At the end of each inhale breath wait until there is a natural need for exhalation, enjoying the peace of the breathless state. As soon as each exhale naturally flows out, mentally chant "*Ha*," making no sound or use of the lips or tongue. Like the inhale procedure, wait until there is a desire for exhalation, all the while enjoying the peace of the breathless state (*aho 'ole*). When breath flows in again, mentally chant "*Alo*" for the duration of the in-flowing breath. When the breath naturally goes out again, without force or act of will, mentally chant "*Hā*" until it is fully out.

Continue repeating the *Alo- Hā* procedure as long as you want or feel the need. When you are proficient at this, you will start to recognize yourself as a soul. You will realize that you are the consciousness and intelligence in the body.

KUKULU 'O KE AO: Pillar of Light

This technique involves the practice of *Hā* (essence of life), which focuses on the exhalation part of respiration. Before beginning, surround yourself with a light silver color for protection. Then visualize a three-dimensional teardrop about the size of a pea in the middle of your heart area. On the exhalation, send this symbol down through the spinal column and out the tailbone down to the core of "Mother" earth. The earth's energetic color in this case is copper, which is not visible to most of us in this dimensional frequency. On the exhalation, draw into your teardrop symbol the copper energies from Mother Earth's *piko* (center). On the next *Hā*, bring your teardrop up through your spine to a position 3 feet above your head with its copper cord attached to the earth's core. With the next exhalation, expand your copper cord to just outside the diameter of your body. Take a deep breath then on exhale, draw into your surroundings and into every cell in your body Earth's healing color of copper.

Visualize a second teardrop in the heart area and on exhalation, send it up to the center of "Father" sun. On exhalation draw into this teardrop the gold energetic frequency of the sun. On the next exhalation, send this teardrop via the spine to a place 12 inches below your feet with its gold cord attached to the center of the sun. With the next exhalation, expand your gold cord to just outside the diameter of your body. With the next exhalation, draw into your surroundings and into every cell in your body the Sun's healing color of gold. You now have the frequency of light silver/copper/gold (tri-metal) energies surrounding you and saturating every cell in your body for protection and healing.

Some benefits of Kukulu 'O Ke Ao.

- Helps to activate or reset your personal 'piko' (chakras).
- Activates DNA strand potential.
- Helps you to transmit non-distorted frequencies resulting in a more powerful and longer lasting (if not permanent) healing.
- Protects you from "disharmonic" energies of infiltration.
- Amplifies or expands the results of spiritual work.
- Harmonizes personal and environmental energies (realigns disharmonic frequencies in the body to their perfect natural order).
- Helps to retain the stream of higher frequency energies flowing through our universe and our planet.

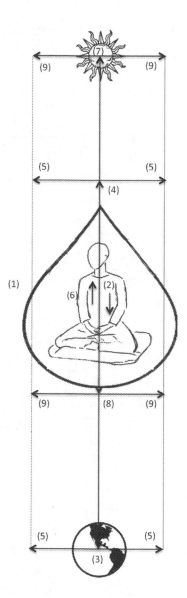

Kukulu o ke au

Note: Each action listed is done on the exhalation (Ha).

1. Surround yourself with a light silver color of protection.
2. Visualize a three dimensional teardrop in the heart area then take it down to the center of Mother Earth via your spine.
3. Fill this teardrop with the copper color of Mother Earth.
4. Bring teardrop up through spine to a place 3 feet above your head with a copper color cord connected to center of Mother Earth.
5. Expand this copper cord to surround the outside of your body.
6. Take a new teardrop from your heart area up to the center of Father Sun.
7. Fill this teardrop with the color of Gold.
8. Bring teardrop with gold cord through spine to a place 1 foot below your body.
9. Expand the gold cord to surround the outside of your body.

Benefits of Kukulu 'o ke ao

- Triggers DNA activation
- Increases healing frequency
- Protects from "disharmonic" energies of infiltration
- Amplifies (spiritual) intentions
- Harmonizes personal and environmental energies
- Helps to hold the flow of higher frequency energies

MAMAO AKU OLA

Sending healing energies to another person (distance healing).

This technique is ideal after the *kukulu 'o ke ao*. Visualize or create a light silver ball of energy the size of a pea that is expandable. On exhalation draw the earth's copper current and the sun's gold current simultaneously (frequency energy) into the heart chakra (*piko pu'uwai*) via the spinal cord, into this ball. On exhalation repeat this process and expand the ball to the size of a golf ball. Then repeat this process and expand the ball to the size of a baseball. Repeat again and expand the ball to the size of softball. Continue until the ball is surrounding the house or building you are meditating in. If you are outside, then it can be as big as you want it to be. Next, on exhalation, compress or squeeze the ball back down to the size of a pea into the *piko pu'uwai*. On the next exhalation, send this silver/copper/gold ball of radiant healing light into the heart chakra of the person you want to help (in their healing process). On the final inhalation, draw the earth's and sun's energy up to your heart area continuing on to the other person's heart chakra, and on exhalation (*Ha* breath) burst the ball of light so that all of this healing light (energy) radiates through every cell within the person's body. Finally, envision only vibrant healthy tissues throughout the person's body.

Practice both procedures daily at specific times throughout the day until the healing process is complete. With practice this can take just a few minutes each time you do it. When you feel comfortable doing the *kukulu 'o ke ao*, go out and teach others who are willing to commit to the process, and have them join the group. Remember, there can be no sympathy or sadness in this circle, as it slows down the healing process. The group must envision healing for the person they are helping and focus solely on the end result, which is a strong, healthy, functional, and youthful, body, mind and soul.

OVERVIEW OF MAMAO AKU OLA (Tri-Metals)

1. Visualize and create a light silver expandable ball (the size of a pea) of radiant healing energies into your *piko pu'uwai* (heart chakra) on exhalation.
2. Draw earth's copper energy and sun's gold energy into this ball on *Ha*.
3. Repeat the breathing technique and expand the ball to the size of a golf ball.
4. Repeat the breathing technique and expand the ball to the size of a baseball.
5. Repeat the breathing technique and expand the ball to the size of softball.
6. Keep increasing the size until it is the size of a basketball, a beach ball, the size of your house, the size of your town.
7. Shrink the ball back to the size of a pea into the heart area.
8. Repeat and send this ball to another person's heart chakra.
9. Draw the earth's copper and sun's gold energy into your heart area and continue to the other person's heart area. Exhale and burst this healing ball of light so radiant energy flows throughout the other person's body.
10. Finally, see only a strong, healthy, functional, and youthful, body, mind and soul for the person you are helping, or for yourself.

HĀ 'EHIKU: Seven breaths

In this meditation technique you have the option to input a positive mantra that supports your focused outcome. List seven words that best describe your envisioned outcome with "I am" or "I have" preceding it. For example, "I am love, grateful, happy, healthy, financially and spiritually abundant." Another example, "I have a strong, healthy, functional, youthful, body, mind, and soul." On the inhalation breath, visualize each word you have listed (approximately seven seconds) then on the hold portion, visualize it again. On the next exhalation do the same thing and finally on the next hold (breath) do it again. Repeat this process seven times.

When doing this meditation technique, allow the breath to naturally flow through either your nose or mouth or both, whatever feels most comfortable. With eyes closed, continue to focus your eyes between the eyebrows.

Overview of ha 'ehiku

o   Inhale slowly for seven seconds
o   Hold for seven seconds
o   Exhale slowly for seven seconds
o   Hold for seven seconds
o   Repeat this process seven times

Another option is to visualize a positive outcome. For example, "Divine healing enters every cell in my body" on the inhalation. Continue positive thoughts during the holding pattern. Give thanks on the exhalation part.

KA LEO O KE KAI

Literally, *ka leo o ke kai* means "the sound or voice of the ocean." This meditation technique involves pressing the tragus of the ear (lobe) onto the external auditory canal with you thumbs. It's like an ear lid that can close the canal inside the ear, which will quiet mind-diverting sounds during deep concentration. When done correctly with deep concentration, you will begin to hear the musical vibratory sounds of the subtle astral centers in the spine.

You'll need a small table or desk that is as high as your chest. Lay a pillow or cushion on the table and place both elbows on it. You should be in a comfortable position while reaching your ear lobes with your thumbs. Be sure your spine and head is in a straight upright position. Your spine must be erect. If you need, put more pillows under your elbow until you have the right height to reach your ears. During this meditation the thumbs tend to loosen their pressure so at the onset use enough pressure to close the opening of the ear comfortably with the lobe. Your objective is to close off outside sounds as much as possible.

While your thumbs are pressing on the ear lobes, place your fingers gently over your closed eyelids, at the outside corners or the inside corners. Your eyeballs should be focused above and between the eyebrows. Keep your gaze at this point where your minds eye (*hokule'a*) exists. It may take some time to do this comfortably, but eventually you may see a few lights or a main central light. If you do see a light, concentrate on it.

By concentrating on any light that you see, you are preparing to see the astral light through the "spiritual eye." It looks like a bright white light with a dark round spot inside it and a star inside that. Along with this, concentrate on the harmonious vibratory sounds of the subtle astral "*piko*" (chakra) sounds in the spine via the ears.

There are variations of sounds vibrating from different cerebrospinal centers (*piko*), of the spine:

- The coccygeal center or the base of the spine has a hum like a bumblebee
- The sacral center has a flute-like sound
- The lumbar center has a harp-like sound
- The thoracic center has a bell-like sound
- The cervical center has a sound of rushing water
- The medulla oblongata has all the sounds of *na piko* (centers) at the same time. It is like the sound of the ocean roaring towards land. It is this symphony of sound that you are seeking to hear.

Meditation is about becoming one with the soul; it is learning to disconnect from physical limitations and remembering the power you have within. When you begin to relate yourself to the soul you begin to be more aware of your past experiences and your connection to *Kumukahi*. In *Kumukahi* you will find all the memory and experiences of your life. Through this inner contact, the veil is lifted to the forgotten past and the realization of your true power will return to your consciousness. Meditation guides you to remember who you really are, eternal and one with *Kumukahi*. When not meditating, you connect to the physical self and its limitations, but in meditation the reverse is true. In meditation you drop the consciousness of the body and remember who you truly are, and then return to have better control of your physical body.

I am awake and realize my true connection to Kumukahi
and my soul and the power I have within.

Notes

CHAPTER 15

Overview of Na'auao Ola Hawaii
A brief summary

Health is the natural functioning of normal life for all humans. In traditional Hawaiian medicinal practices, there is a common understanding about a Principle of Life in the universe that is of Living Substance from which all things are made. This Living Substance exists within us, around us and throughout our universe. This invisible natural energy system or state of being is in and through all forms, and all forms are made of it.

This Universal Living Substance is a conscious thinking substance from which all forms originate. When this Universal Intelligence thinks of a form, it manifests this form; when it thinks of a motion it causes the motion. This Intelligence is always thinking so it is constantly creating, moving toward a fuller and more complete expression of itself. This means creating a more complete life and a more perfect functioning body. This Universal Living Substance only knows perfect health for all and as long as we consciously tap into to this Source, we can manifest perfect health for ourselves. We also have the power within us to separate ourselves from this power through our thoughts creating imbalances within us.

When a person thinks only thoughts of perfect health, the eventual outcome is the internal process manifesting a perfectly healthy body. Therefore, the first step towards perfect health must be to form a concept of being perfectly healthy. Add to this all efforts from any external input (i.e., positive lifestyle changes) that support being a perfectly healthy person. When forming this concept, all thought and action must be committed to this outcome while severing any and all thoughts related to disease and illnesses or doubt.

In developing the concept of health, it is essential to consistently think of or visualize what it would feel like to live and work as if you were perfectly healthy and strong. Imagine yourself doing things the way a healthy person would until you have a fairly good feel of what that would be like. Let your mental and physical actions be in harmony with this conceptual outcome. Let your thoughts be *pono* with your intended outcome so that your body will be in that state of consciousness. "*Oki* everything you do not want including doubt, and embrace everything you do want. Develop a concept of a healthy body, mind, and spirit and let all your actions, your words and your attitude act in alignment with this idea.

Watch your words each and every day. Let your words be in harmony with a healthy body, mind and soul. For example, instead of saying, "I didn't sleep well last night," say "I am looking forward to having a good night's sleep tonight." Instead of "I had," or "I have cancer," perhaps "I am on the road to wellness," would be a better alternative. Another option is "I am progressing rapidly." Disconnect with any thoughts of disease or illness and align yourself with only thoughts of a healthy body, mind and spirit. This also means not being with people that cannot support you 100%.

> *Be one with your thoughts, words, and actions of having a healthy, body, mind and spirit. Disconnect any thoughts, words or actions that link to disease, illness or doubt.*

Having thoughts of only health with absolute *na'au pono* and taking action by positive lifestyle changes, we can cause the Principle of Health within us to become constructively active to the point where disease and illness cannot exist. We can receive additional *mana* from the Universal Principle of Life (*Kumukahi*) by *na'au pono*. By accepting or welcoming this Principle of Life with abundant gratitude for the unlimited health it gives us, *na'au pono* becomes stronger.

A person cannot rely on thoughts of perfect health only; he or she must make positive lifestyle changes that support this outcome. These voluntary functions are eating, drinking, breathing, thinking and sleeping.

Health is the result of thinking and acting in a *pono* way. If a sick person begins to think and act in this way, the Principle of Health within him or her will activate all the internal forces that lead to breaking the blueprint to all diseases. This Principle of Health is the same in all human beings and is related to the Life Principle of the universe. It is able to heal every disease and be activated whenever a person thinks and acts in accordance with the principles and practices of Na'auao Ola Hawaii. Therefore, every person can and will attain perfect health through perseverance.

Mahalo Nui Loa (thank you for listening),
Maka'ala Yates D.C.
Ambassador at Large
Minister of Health
Polynesian Kingdom of Atooi

www.manalomi.com
www.indigenousbotanicals.net
www.buddhablends.com
manaola@centurylink.net
manalomi.my@gmail.com

Notes

Supplemental Health Ideas

Articles and ideas written by Maka'ala

Contents

'Oli Kumukahi	Kumukahi Chant
E aloha Kumukahi ea ea E aloha Kumukahi e	Love to the One Source.
Kumukahi Kumukahi ea ea Kumukahi Kumukahi e	The One Source indeed.
Ho'o (*long*) pono pono ea ea Ho'o (*long*) pono pono e	Living in balance.
Ho'ona'au pono (*long*) ea ea Ho'ona'au pono (*long*) e	Trust, knowing, intuition.
Ho'omana'o pono (*long*) ea ea Ho'omana'o pono (*long*) e	Will Power.
Ho'o (*long*) maika'i ea ea Ho'o (*long*) maika'i c	Gratitude.
No'o no'o pono (*long*) ea ea No'o no'o pono (*long*) e	Discipline.
Mahalo Kumukahi ea ea Mahalo Kumukahi e	Thankful.

Note: Above (*long*) means to hold the previous tone longer.

To listen to this chant and the song version, please visit www. manalomi.com or on YouTube under Maka'ala Yates.

Understanding Hawaiians

It is the year 2012 and the Polynesian Kingdom of Atooi (PKOA) is finally recognized by the United Nations as an indigenous sovereign nation. After many years of painstaking struggle, we, as Hawaiians, can finally return home. The government of Atooi now has jurisdiction over the U.S. government, occupying Hawaii according to international law and the recognition by the UN. You can find the headquarters of this nation on the island of Kauai. The Ali'i Nui (High Chief) is Aleka (Dayne) Aipoalani (a direct descendant of Kaumuali'i) and the kingdom's website is www.atooination.com. PKOA is composed of peoples from diverse cultures whose relationships share the mission of ho'opono 'aina (to make right with the land). Hawaiians now have an opportunity to regain their stolen lands and government (1893 colonial possession by the U.S).

Atooi is a far cry from my young days growing up on the Big Island of Hawaii, when land was continually swindled from the Hawaiian people by the corrupt practices of the new invaders. My father knew every Hawaiian living in West Hawaii on the Big Island and knew that these people never sold or gave their land to anyone. I believe the term he used was "adverse possession." This is when an individual or a group pays taxes on a specific parcel of land, and after seven years, can claim that land if no one else has paid taxes on it. You can look it up in Black's law dictionary for a more detailed description. Of course, Hawaiians never knew or were told about this new law.

When my father was attending Kamehameha School on Oahu (an all Hawaiian elementary and high school) he was reprimanded every time he spoke Hawaiian, his first language. English was forced upon the native people of Hawaii (*Kanaka Maoli*) as well as a new foreign culture and religion. The point is if you want to eradicate a culture, you first take their land away, then their language.

In order for the Hawaiians to survive the events of the past, they were forced to form organizations based on Western systems of thought that were confusing to them. To survive the restructuring of their way of life, they had to adapt. They had to have representation in this new order, to protect and defend what little they had left.

This was the beginning of an unhealthy seed of exploitation being planted on sacred land. Today there are many Hawaiian organizations that carry the signature of an idea of a democratic organization that is based on a wrongful form of democracy. These pseudo Hawaiian organizations are using the same model that our ancestors had seen practiced against them and their *'aina hiwahiwa* (precious land). There is a deep history of self-interest, greed, and political corruption that we have experienced by a country that turns an eye on its own sacred ideals as stated in the American Constitution.

An example of this is Bishop Estate, which controls lands, worth more than 6 billion dollars. The original intention of Bishop Estate was for the education of native Hawaiians. Bernice Pauahi Paki, the great granddaughter of Kamehameha I, married Charles Reed Bishop and together they created a trust for the Hawaiian children. Unfortunately, today Bishop Estate is filled with a dark history of corruption, nepotism and greed. My uncle who was a surveyor for a private company noticed many instances where Bishop Estate encroached on other Hawaiian lands by moving the boundary markers.

For anyone looking in from the outside, you can start to understand how challenging it is for a Hawaiian to develop a clear sense of his or her own identity. We were told in many ways and in many forms that if we are to survive in the new world we had to let go of our traditions. We had to let go of a fairly complex system of deep understanding that people and government did not own land, but that land was a precious gift from the gods (*Kumukahi*). As a young man, my father always taught me that our *kuleana* (responsibility) to the land is to perpetuate it for future generations where people and nature prospered harmoniously.

Imagine what went through my *na kupuna* (parent's, grandparent's, ancestor's) mind when a foreign government came in and took them over, against their will! This new colonial invader then introduced a new system of land management. Land was now to be divided amongst those that wished "private ownership" for personal gain. They also introduced "government ownership" for personal gain. How were the Hawaiians to react when these private individuals became government officials creating laws that served their own personal interests? The new Hawaii perpetuated money, power and profit with no concern for the people or the land. It created a wound to the spirit of the people whose heart and soul was deeply rooted to the sacred land and sea. It has taken Hawaiians many generations to digest and realize just what this wounding has meant to them, and to the land that they love. Today, almost half of all Hawaiians live outside of Hawaii mostly because they can't afford to live on their ancestral land.

In 1778 it was estimated that about 400,000 Hawaiians lived throughout the islands of Hawaii. One hundred years later in 1878 this population decreased to about 40,000 people due, in large part, to diseases introduced by contact with foreigners. These diseases included venereal disease, smallpox, measles, whooping cough and influenza.

I remember my sister and I, as young kids, trekking along the cliffs of Ka'awaloa (near where my ancestors came from) finding a small cave with eight children's bones neatly wrapped individually in tapa cloth. We both wondered what happened to them and why so many in one spot? I realize now that it was probably one of the diseases that killed so many in such a short period of time. Imagine the impact this might have on you and your family. It could have been my relatives buried in that unmarked grave. I can't imagine the deep sadness I would feel to lose so many people who were so precious to me. When you value family as a source of joy and renewal, it becomes a serious loss, a deep wound, especially if it is your own children.

Add to these deep wounds to the spirit of the people, the introduction of a new religion. A religion that tells the host culture that traditional customs, dances and ceremonies are immoral and blasphemous. They were told to turn their other cheek, to be passive and forgive those who have ruined their way of life. It is interesting to note that the five biggest landowners in Hawaii today are descendants of missionaries. To add insult to injury, the Hawaiians must forget their own language, their own customs, and their own sacred traditions.

It has been a long struggle with incredible odds to find our voices and to regain our own identity. Today we are experiencing a non-religious spiritual renaissance, a reconnection to our true past from the pre-warrior period. In 1976 when I sailed on the double hull canoe "Hokule'a," I didn't realize that it was to become the turning point for us as *Kanaka Maoli*, to heed the calling of our ancestors and our lands. It became the reawakening of our consciousness and the resurrection of our voices and sacred traditions that were buried with our *na kupuna* generations ago. It is the *aloha* (love) of our people, the Hawaiians and those that are Hawaiian at heart, that will bring harmony and peace to the *'aina* and the *na kanaka* for generations to come. It is the heart of Aloha that is unique to Hawaii's secret past, buried deep in the heart and souls of those who love the land. This is Hawaii's true calling and its gift to the world.

Mahalo.

Indigenous Medicine Mindset

"Health is a matter of wisdom," says *Kupuna* Hale, one of my Hawaiian elder teachers, not scientific knowledge. She further expressed to me that what I was learning in the "scientific" school of thought (pre-med and Chiropractic) is considered child's science as compared to our ancestors.

The scientific medical view of disease is that disease is centered in the body. The Indigenous Polynesian's view of a so-called disease or illness is an imbalance of the soul, a disconnection of meaning, of purpose, of essence. The task of the *Kahuna Lapa'au* (in this case, a master in Hawaiian medicine) is to heal the soul from its disconnection, to aid in bringing the soul back to the One. Our modern society is riddled with lost and disconnected souls.

The *Kahuna Lapa'au* recognizes each soul as sacred and always connected to *Kumukahi* (One Source). They viewed life (living) as a spiritual practice, not a dogmatic religion or other mind-controlling system. Bringing health back into balance was a spiritual practice. Therefore, based on the mindset of the ancient Hawaiian medicine *kahuna*, disease is caused by the disconnection of the soul in one form or another. Living an empty life, which is living without meaning or with meaning that is too trivial or too materialistic for the needs of a sacred soul is a form of disconnection. I feel that Western culture has purposely persuaded us to shut our eyes to the truth. It feels as if we have abandoned the feminine principle. We have lost sight to who or what we truly are - sacred beings living on sacred ground connected to *Kumukahi*.

The feminine way is one of understanding the world, a way of finding solutions that affect the whole, and a way of taking action for the highest good for all. To have a sacred experience requires a balance of our feminine capacity. It's valuing the individual: the intuitive, the character of the person. It allows us to dive deeper down the rabbit-hole (not just focusing on the surface of things). Don't get me wrong; I am not about getting rid of the masculine principle especially when it pertains to healing. I am for reclaiming wholeness, and integrity.

Below is a Hawaiian chant of empowerment that I have modified to include all people.

E iho ana 'o luna	-	What is above is brought down
E pi'i ana 'o lalo	-	What is below is lifted up
E hui ana ka honua	-	The world is united
Ikaika ko kakou 'uhane	-	Our Spirit remains strong
Imua ka lahui na po'e kanaka a pau loa	-	Let us all move forward together (as one wind)

The imbalance in the western medical system is the over emphasis on a masculine principal approach that permeates our entire culture. This essentially belittles all of those that are brave enough to ask questions. It lessens the integrity and soul connection of the people that operate within that system and it diminishes the self-confidence of the people who seek out that system for their health care needs. When you enter a typical doctor's office, there is an immediate sense of disconnect, a sense of diminished self-power. Granted, some of this is self-induced, but much of it is the sterile environment of the office. There is literature littered throughout the waiting room and pharmaceutical advertising reminding us of our individual limitations to bring health back into balance. It feels more like a business than a relationship to heal a sacred soul. "How will you be paying for this?" "Do you have insurance to pay for today's visit?" When you eventually see a doctor, rarely is there any physical contact (except from the nurse perhaps) and lucky you if you happen to get an eye contact! When you leave the doctor's office, you may feel even less capable, even though you have been given the correct diagnosis and treatment protocols. When you experience a strong masculine principle style, you feel the doctor's strength, the doctor's dominance. Even if you are helped, you end up feeling lesser of a sacred person.

When someone interacts with you from the feminine side of themselves, you feel empowered, you feel your unique self, the full capacity of your possibilities. Every medical *Kahuna* understood this balance and the importance of establishing a relationship with their patients including the connection with the treatment protocol or medicinal prescription. Imagine if the Western medical system was like this, as well as providing the right diagnoses and treatment protocols.

We no longer need a disease-centered medical system. We need a form of health care that embraces the interdependence of all living things. What we need is an indigenous medicine mindset approach based on relationships that are *pono*.

My father always reminded me about how the little words, not the big ones, that can make a difference in a just relationship between two people. Complex and foreign words unfamiliar to the general community can cause a separation between people. The medical field has conveniently developed a communication system that encourages their separation from the general public. Their scientific language makes others feel less than competent and perhaps helps them feel superior to the layperson. There is absolutely no reason why those in the medical profession can't use a language everyone can understand. The medical profession has created a masculine principle of what some call a "practice of professional isolation." Maybe we should start the healing process by first healing the professional isolation? We definitely need to change medicine from a culture of competition, independence and separation. The masculine system can prescribe and possibly cure (a legal term only they can use), but the feminine principle heals the soul.

Mahalo.

Daily Ho'oponopono Practice

Relationships: Correcting Your Mistakes

Your relationship to others should have more value than the need to be right. Accepting responsibility for an offense, or mistake that you have made, and expressing regret for the wrong that was done, is essential for a long lasting relationship. Doing it in a truthful manner and committing not to do it again is a critical part of repairing a mistake.

Don't wait to correct a mistake, do it immediately! Many of us delay correcting a mistake, due largely in fear of the consequences. Some may be unaware that they have offended another person, while others just don't know how to correct the mistake.

Growing up in Hawaii as kids, we were always taught by example how to immediately correct any wrong toward others. It never felt forced. No one demanded that we do the right thing. It was the way of life growing up in Honaunau, Kona. Seeing the positive outcome was reward enough for us to understand the right thing to do.

My son, at the age of nine, was already practicing correcting mistakes or making right what was wronged. I like to think that he got this from observing my wife and I correcting our mistakes with each other in a gentle and kind way. His cousin was visiting us for a week and upon returning home complained to his mom that my son broke his toy. Overhearing my wife and her sister on the phone discussing this angered my son because he felt he was innocent. I remember him shouting, "I didn't do it, Mom!" Minutes later he called his cousin to discuss how his cousin put the toy on his shelf, which accidently fell and landed on the floor. I could hear my son say, "Maybe it broke then?" I think the conversation took less than five minutes when I overheard my son saying, "No problem, I love you too." Dealing with correcting complex mistakes is easier when you are raised with this concept from a very young age.

I understand the apprehension some people may have in owning up to their mistakes. It takes courage and humility to correct a wrong. It is the right thing to do for the sake of those we have offended. It's also healthy for the mistaken to rectify the conflict. The outcome is a healthy dose of self-awareness, which keeps us accountable and brings clarity so we don't have to repeat the same mistake again. I remember my father telling me when I was playing tennis on my high school varsity team in the 60's, "An unintelligent mistake is when you repeat the same mistake over and over. An intelligent mistake is when you don't repeat the same mistake twice." I took this to heart and have been applying this idea to everything in my life.

Accepting the fact that you have done something wrong, melts away ego and allows for self-correcting. A strong soul is one that doesn't need to strive for perfection, but one that recognizes when their mistake hurt others. A strong soul is one who takes responsibility for one's actions, expresses one's wrongdoing, and never repeats the action again.

Admitting our mistakes is not easy for some, but the cost for the alternative – denial, hiding from the truth, deception – is far more costly. I have often seen patients in my clinic suffering from a debilitating condition that had some hint of someone causing a mistaken situation on them, or vice versa. Holding on to or living with an old mistake is not healthy at all. The first step in correcting any wrongdoing is to take the initiative to acknowledge you created the mistake. When you do this, you are taking responsibility for your actions. Doing something with meaningful commitment is the foundation for an integrated or a harmonious life. It builds integrity when done from the heart. Eliminate any excuses, and don't take things personally when there is no response from the person one has wronged. Having pure intentions when making things right puts a higher value on the rekindling of a relationship.

The next step is to undo what you did. "Owning up" to your actions, or behavior, indicates that what you did was wrong and you are asking "what can I do to make it right?" Your body language, facial expression, and tone of voice should be consistent with your words and heart. Let your intentions on the inhale breath be *pono* with your words on the exhale breath. Your intentions should be for the highest good for all parties concerned. Watch and choose your words wisely. Eliminate words such as, "if, but, I want to, and using a passive voice.

Finally, cut the energy cord to the entire incident. Transmute this energy by surrounding it with a white light. Recycle this transmuted energy into the air (universe, ethers). Create a positive mantra for the outcome such as, I am love, we are love, our relationship is a positive loving one, etc.

There are a few things that are very real: accidents, human flaws, and forgiveness. The first two may be out of our control so we must do our best with the third. The purpose of correcting our mistakes is to build upon a sustainable, healthy, and rich community of supportive citizens. Honoring each other and practicing self-awareness may not be easy at first, but one thing is certain--you can't lose by correcting a mistake.

Mahalo.

Aumakua

Like many Hawaiian words and ideas, the many layers of the term *aumakua* are quite extensive. On the surface it literally means ancestor gods, the god spirits of those who were in life, spiritual ancestors, a benevolent guardian spirit or family protector. As you penetrate the deeper surfaces of *aumakua* without influences from modern religious ideas, you begin to realize the boundless possibilities it bears. For example, it describes how from one becomes two and two becomes four and so forth. It describes the makeup of the time construct that we live in and the idea that frequency is the combination of oscillation and vibration, *aumakua po and aumakua ao.*

> *If our lives have been worthy, our aumakua will be waiting to welcome us. Then we too shall inhabit the eternal realm of the ancestor spirits. We in our time shall become aumakua to our descendants even yet unborn.*
> Mary Kawena Pukui
> Nana I Ke Kumu

The concept of *aumakua* is based on the close relationships of the *'ohana* (family) and their spiritual ancestors. Through the family's *aumakua*, a human-to-spirit communication was possible and a family was better able to pass on prayers to *Kumukahi*. A*umakua* can take on an invisible form or a visible one because of their ability to take *kino lau* (many bodies, many forms). These forms were either *aumakua po* or *aumakua ao*.

Today, most of Hawaii's multicultural population has either forgotten the *aumakua* or has never known it. For some, *aumakua* is a childhood memory. I remember my father taking me out into the ocean to feed a very specific granddaddy of a shark in Kona, Hawaii. By taking care of his *aumakua*, he in return received an abundance of fish. One form of *aumakua* that is prevalent with me today is the *pueo* (Hawaiian owl). It is always around me when I send out a prayer to my ancestors and *Kumukahi*.

Kumu: A Title of Fact,
Fiction or Distraction?

In the past, it was very respectful to address a teacher of a particular profession in Hawaii as *Kumu*. Traditionally, it was an identifier given by a community to a master teacher who carried on the responsibilities of their profession. It was an honor given to this master by the collective, based on that person's abilities and connection to their community. Part of the teacher's responsibility was to offer their expertise to the needs of the community and in return the community provided whatever support the *Kumu* required.

Today, I am seeing more and more people identifying themselves as *Kumu* "so and so" or *Kumu* of "this or that." This is especially true when it comes to teaching a form of Hawaiian healing class. Perhaps the term *Kumu* has evolved into a title of authority. I've often wondered, does the title make the person or does the person make the title? Why do we need a title in the first place? Who assigns these titles anyway? None of my Hawaiian healing teachers ever called themselves a *Kumu* nor did they advertise themselves as a *Kumu*. They neither demanded nor required that they be addressed as a *Kumu*. This is also true with the recognition as a *Kahuna*. So why is there a noticeable increase in the word *Kumu* in front of someone's name? Some of them are Hawaiians and some are non-Hawaiians. Is there a school of Hawaiian healing that certifies these people that I don't know about? Is there a revised system of traditional Kumu-ism that is being revisited? What's going on? I know there are protocols within the *hula* (traditional Hawaiian dance) groups, but within the Hawaiian healing circles that I have been involved in, it's much different. Learning to assist in the healing of the body, mind and soul requires lifetime of experience.

Kumu is a term usually used in the context within the Hawaiian culture although not limited to it. Some examples are; *Kumu Hula* - a teacher of hula; *Kumu Lomi* - a teacher of *lomilomi*; *Kumu La'au Lapa'au* - a teacher of herbal medicine; and *Kumu Haha* - a teacher of diagnostics or medical intuition.

The word *kumu* has many translations. It refers to a red fish (goat fish), a trunk of a tree, a source or origin of something, a sweetheart, good looking, foundation, title (as to land or position), a purpose or reason, and a name of a variety of red stalked taro.

I have been involved in the Hawaiian healing ways since the age of six. In all those years not once did any of my Hawaiian teachers require that they be addressed as a *Kumu* or promoted themselves as a *Kumu*. It was not something that they aspired to either within their community or within a certain profession. I should mention, however, that up to a certain point in the evolution of the Hawaiian people, children went through a selection process to carry on a particular profession. It was a lifetime of learning that the child was committed to, but to my knowledge, this has not happened since the early 1900's. This is true in Kona, Hawaii at least.

The basic premise in learning a skill or gaining knowledge especially from a Hawaiian perspective is to have the ability to provide the best service or expertise possible without causing injury or emotional distress to the receivers. The skill or expertise gained can be used for the exchange of energy, be it money, products, services etc.

Why an individual wants to learn something, his or her intention will determine the quality of outcome. For example, taking a class for one's personal agenda versus genuinely wanting to expand one's awareness in healing creates two entirely different outcomes. In my thirty plus years of teaching Hawaiian medicine and modalities, I have seen those with personal agendas falter with limited success. Those who applied their studies for the greater-good almost always sustained financial success as well as growth in wisdom. Going into a *lomi* class with the idea of teaching the course soon after takes away from the potential of being the best practitioner possible. Whether you see the correlation or not, the fact is from a Hawaiian indigenous mindset, you must have experience just to become a good practitioner. From time to time I have seen a few students from my class and other Hawaiian teacher's class return to their hometown and immediately offer the same class as if they were experts. In the early 80's a student of Aunty Margaret Machado wrote a book on *lomi* verbatim from Auntie's notes. She did this the same year she took the class. In my sixteen years with Aunty Margaret, not once did I ever consider becoming a teacher. It was later in life that the community-at-large expressed the need for me to carry forward the knowledge and wisdom handed down from a lineage of Hawaiian healers.

The role of the teacher is to help students strengthen their sense of responsibility. The role of the student is to help the teacher lighten that load. It is a key element in the relationship between student (*Haumana*) and teacher. It is a connection that lightens as it strengthens. Sadly, a few so called, "*Kumu*" mislead many followers with embellished information and fictitious or no lineage connection to a Hawaiian source. I can see why it is so hard to find the "real deal." How can anyone become a teacher just by taking one class? The "rabbit hole" goes very deep in Hawaiian healing concepts and modalities. I know some of my Hawaiian teachers questioned the integrity of a few self-proclaimed *na Kumu* (teachers). In Aunty Margaret's words, "what are they teaching?"

Often I am asked, how does one find a true teacher of Hawaiian healing knowledge? How will I recognize him or her? Can you point me in the right direction? Aunty Margaret was unique. She practiced what she taught and taught what she practiced. A teacher should live his or her talk and talk what he or she lives. It is about continuous practice of expansion and self-study. For a teacher, the student is never wrong or slow or inept. When I hear a teacher complain about a student, I think there is trouble with that teacher. There is a famous quote by William Arthur Ward: "The mediocre teacher tells, the superior teacher demonstrates, the great teacher inspires." If the student does not understand the information given, then the teacher must inquire within as to how to better impart that knowledge. What other avenues can be used to explain a concept. Creativity is a key ingredient in the bag of tools available to the teacher.

The bond between a *haumana* and a *Kumu* is like two outrigger canoes in the open ocean, each filled with paddlers and a steersman. If the canoe in the back gets close enough to the lead canoe, it can assist that canoe by pushing it forward from the wake it creates at its bow. As long as the lead canoe keeps its momentum going forward the rear canoe can assist its progress. The rear canoe represents the *Kumu* and the lead canoe represents *na haumana*. I like this metaphor because it suggests the deep bond of trust that must exist between teacher and student. The more the student advances, the more the teacher can give to the student. I have always felt the nudging by my teachers in my voyage of learning and I still feel them long after they have left this world.

The teacher's entire responsibility is to the student. Their role is to help each student evolve to their highest potential. There is no agenda to mold a student according to the teacher's ideas or purpose. The teacher can provide a safe environment by holding sacred space. This allows the opportunity to guide the student with tools beyond the subject matter of the class or workshop.

My role as a teacher is one that encourages the waking of our group consciousness so each individual can see what his or her true potential can be. There are only a handful of instructors in the Mana Lomi® organization and every two years we get together to share and discuss how we can better ourselves as teachers in the work of Hawaiian healing principles and concepts. We don't look down or up at anyone, but rather "eye to eye."

We are all students of life. Let us be who we are, no more and no less.

Mahalo.

Mana Lomi ®
Problem Solving Hawaiian Bodywork Therapy

ML Philosophy

The vision of ML is grounded in the ancient Hawaiian principles of the *ahupuaʻa* "pre warrior" period. In this philosophy we embrace the idea that everything in this world is an embodiment of Supreme Consciousness, which at its essence pulsates with love and life. It is a concept of pursuing sustainable-community-building.

ML is a hands-on Hawaiian bodywork therapy that has the ability to communicate deep within the bones of the individual, which allows the practitioner to connect to the soul of that person. This concept gives room to allow the practitioner to go as deeply as the client can tolerate, yet be non-invasive, while achieving the desired outcome. The ML practitioner uses a multitude of techniques that affect the golgi tendon organ (GTO), muscle spindle fibers and the pain receptors. It is an integrative approach (stepping out of the box) of Hawaiian healing in which the precise therapeutic science of ML is blended with a balance of biomechanics and problem solving skills.

ML has a unique system of linking the old Hawaiian healing techniques into a modern world. It is spiritually inspiring, heart and mind opening and yet grounded in a deep knowledge of problem-solving therapeutics. In the right hands it can be one of the most therapeutically effective and physically transformative styles of Hawaiian healing.

The central philosophy of ML is that each person is equally divine in every aspect – body, mind & soul. We see each other eye to eye. No one is above another and no one is below another. The concept of evaluating the constitution of the whole person and its imbalances allows the ML practitioner to look at each client as a unique individual.

The highest intention of practicing ML is to align with *Kumukahi* (One Source). As we deepen our alignment with *Kumukahi*, we step deeper into the flow of love and kindness. Tapping into this higher knowledge of possibilities, fuels our deepest vision--to lovingly embrace the creative flow of life through each breath and intentions in our ML practice.

In each class we creatively offer our individual light and our unique rhythm with the genuine prayer of adding more love and beauty to the world.

The art of ML is a co-participation with *Kumukahi*, our clients and us as practitioners – ML is not a practice of unilateral healing, subservience or an attempt to control Nature. The physical body is a magnificent manifestation of *Kumukahi*, not some inferior dependent material vessel. Likewise, our thoughts, emotions, and passions are not obstacles to self-awareness.

There is a *Kumu'ike* from which all things are made. It is a force that is omnipresent and fills the interspaces of all things within the universe. It is where all life comes from. The thought from this Source shapes the form and energy of all things that are of this world. The form and energy created are always of perfect function and health. If we as humans think only thoughts of perfect function and health then the outcome is perfect function and health. All the Power of Life will be there to assist in whatever the needs are.

The ML community (*ahupua'a*) is inclusive, life affirming, and evolving. Individuality and creative self-expression, which exemplifies the *ahupua'a*, are encouraged and welcomed. Furthermore, ML encourages a wide variety of spiritual and religious self-expressions, which are heart-centered and cultivate love and happiness. We acknowledge, respect, and invite a diversity of experience both within our own *ahupua'a* and among those outside the community who are seeking to align with the Divine.

The Mana Lomi® technique is available for everyone that is open to learning the Hawaiian ways of healing. We welcome all forms of cultural and ethnic diversity.

E Komo Mai (Welcome)

www.manalomi.com
www.indigenousbotanicals.net
www.buddhablends.com

Wai Ola
Water of Life

Life for Hawaiians, especially before colonization, was centered on water and agriculture (land). The most important food staple at that time was *kalo* (taro), which relied heavily on the *mana* of the water because *kalo* was considered *'ohana* to the Hawaiians. This particular *mana* was established through attentive cleanliness of the river ways and by ceremony, which included *pule* (prayers) by the villagers. These ceremonies and prayers were important in maintaining a positive relationship between land and water, which led to the same relationship to all *Kanaka Maoli*.

There are two kinds of water in the Hawaiian language, *wai* (rain or land water) and *kai* (sea or salt water). The ancient God for *wai* was *Kané* and for the ocean water it was *Kanaloa*. Of the many water ceremonies used in pre-western contact Hawaii, the two most notable were *kapu kai* and *pikai*.

Kapu kai is the ceremonial bathing of one's self in the sea or salt water if on land. This ceremony was done to purify the body and spirit of the individual, especially when an imbalance was present. This type of ritual was usually done in private however; it was not uncommon for a group of villagers or family members to perform *kapu kai* to bring harmony and peace into their *ahupua'a* and ultimately the world.

Ahupua'a (side note)

The original purpose of the *ahupua'a* concept was recognizing that each of us have responsibilities that contribute to the wellness or demise of the community and ultimately, the rest of the living world. The original intent (pre-warrior period) of the *ahupua'a* system was the non-verbal agreement among the inhabitants to protect, preserve and sustain a particular area of land and water that flowed from the mountains to the ocean. The outcome of each responsible action determined the outcome for the individual and ultimately, the people within that community. The island was divided equally like slices of a pie and everyone was allowed to travel the "*mauka-makai*" (highlands and lowlands) routes to access the abundance and to give back to the *ahupua'a*.

Through sharing resources and constantly working within the rhythms of their natural environment, Hawaiians enjoyed abundance and a balanced lifestyle with leisure time for recreation during the harvest season. The system was one of *lokahi*, which was the understanding of, "living as one" or we are all connected. Every thought, word(s) or action had a direct effect on everyone within that *ahupua'a* and ultimately to the planet. The original people were doing their share of maintaining balance and harmony within themselves and their community.

Sometimes *kapu kai* was done as a precautionary measure to ward off negative energies prior to performing in a public event. It was to ensure that the individual was not carrying wrong intentions or allowing wrong energies to interfere in their public presentation. This ceremony was also done prior to a student's hula graduation, which was called *'ailolo* and after a kahuna's healing treatment. Women did this ceremony following the end of their menstrual cycle each month.

Kapu kai should not be confused with *'au'au kai*, which is bathing in the ocean for physical cleanliness. On the Big Island of Hawaii, *kapu kai* was usually done in five consecutive days. It was not uncommon however, to do this ceremony periodically for general improvement of physical and spiritual health. A child or an ill person could be given this ceremonial bath by someone else.

Each year I have a two week intensive Mana Lomi® (Hawaiian problem solving bodywork therapy) program in Hawaii. At least two days prior to everyone arriving I will go to the beach to do a *kapu kai* ceremony to purify myself, and my intentions. I envision everyone having an inspirational, life-changing experience. I see each person achieving exceptional skills that go beyond the mechanics of learning this spiritual and specific bodywork technique. During the ceremony I offer a *ho'okupu* (gift) to the ocean and *Kanaloa*, which consist of Hawaiian herbs wrapped in Hawaiian ti-leaves. I will always end with a Hawaiian chant of inspiration.

Pikai is a traditional Hawaiian ceremony of sprinkling seawater or salt water to purify an area or person from spiritual contamination and harmful energies. This ceremony is commonly confused with the Christian ceremony of sprinkling of water. The use of water in symbolic purification is universal; however, *pikai* during the pre-western contact was unique to Hawaiians. The use of fresh water, seawater and even coconut water was used ceremonially.

Essentially, when the water of purification (*wai huikala*) had sea salt in it, the ceremony was *pikai*. Sometimes *'olena* (turmeric) *or limu kala* (sea vegetable) was added to the seawater for an enhanced outcome. In the hale *pulo'ulo'u* (house of purification sweat ceremony) that I conduct, I like to use *awa* (kava kava), *'olena* and sandalwood (*'ili'ahi*) to reconnect to the real power we have within.

Pikai was done when a new house or a new canoe was completed. As many other rituals do, *pikai* help relieve the feeling of being helpless in an unseen outcome (unknown) or the fear of something. *Pikai* brings a sense of protection from influences felt to be unclean or harmful.

The ancient Hawaiians viewed water as the essence of life for their *ahupua'a* much like their view of the human body. The land like the human body is dependent on the health of the "river of life."

Mahalo

CHD and Cholesterol

It was on a flight from Medford, Oregon to New Haven, CT a few years ago when a strong desire hit me to write about the possibilities of preventing heart problems. I was thinking about a few friends of mine from different parts of the country who had experienced heart attacks and yet had appeared quite healthy when I last saw them.

For many years, medical thinking about heart disease was primarily based on the "lipid hypothesis." This theory proposes that foods high in saturated fat and cholesterol leads to blockages in the arteries to the heart. Cholesterol gets into the arteries in the form of plaque, which over time causes blockages that starve the heart of vital oxygenated blood, often leading to heart attacks. I know I have been out of school (BS in Human Biology and Doctorate in Chiropractic) for some time now so I had to do some digging around to bring me up to speed on preventative measures and the latest thinking regarding heart diseases.

Research and data (CDC/NCHS National Health Survey, 2009) indicate that native Hawaiians suffer some of the worst health outcomes in the State of Hawaii and perhaps in the continental U.S. I feel this is equally true for Polynesians in general. They have one of the highest risk factors for coronary heart disease (CHD).

Some researchers are now questioning the theory and finding serious flaws that "foods rich in saturated fats and cholesterol eventually lead to heart attacks." Heart disease in the U.S. increased during the period when the use of saturated fats decreased. There is evidence showing that children who were on low fat diets and adults who were on cholesterol-lowering drugs, CHD still rose.

If not cholesterol then what's causing heart disease? It's a question that cannot be entirely solved in scientific labs, but perhaps on the front lines working directly with people may help in finding some clues. The clues are all there and you don't have to be a dedicated scientist to figure it out. It is not so complex that the general public cannot make reasonable life-style adjustments based on these common sense clues.

CHD is not from one cause or a single element, but from multiple etiologies. Some of the elements that can contribute to heart disease include damage to heart muscles or valves (congenital effects); inflammation and damage associated with various viral, bacterial, fungal or parasitic diseases. Rheumatic fever or syphilis can lead to heart disease, as can genetic or autoimmune disorders.

According to CDC statistics, heart disease was relatively rare in 1900, accounting for approximately 9% of all deaths in the U.S. (www.cdc. gov/nchs/data/dvs/lead1900_98.pdf).

By 1950, CHD was the leading cause of deaths in the U.S. (48% of all deaths)! It went down to about 38% by 1998, but that could be due to improved surgical procedures (angioplasty, by-pass, etc.).

Some risk factors for heart disease as cited by medical viewpoints include high blood cholesterol, smoking, and lack of exercise, stress, and obesity. There are of course the obvious chemical imbalances and nutrient deficiencies such as vitamin A and D that is not high on their radar screen. Heart researchers for the most part have ignored the possible role that vitamins, minerals and natural foods have in protecting the heart.

Vitamins A and D for example, act as catalysts for protein and mineral assimilation. They support endocrine function and protect against inflammation. Vitamin A is needed to convert cholesterol into steroid hormones, but is depleted by stress. Of course stress contributes to a lot health problems. Cholesterol lowering drugs increases the body's need for vitamin A. Vitamin D helps prevent high blood pressure and protects against spasms. It is needed for calcium absorption, assists in the workings of the body's nervous system and helps prevent arrhythmias.

Vitamin E is an antioxidant that prevents free radicals from causing damage to cells and it plays an essential role in cellular respiration especially in cardiac muscles. It aids the dilation of blood vessels and inhibits coagulation of the blood by preventing clots from forming.

Vitamin C is also an antioxidant and prevents against free radicals and it helps support the integrity of the artery walls. Stress diminishes vitamin C, however. Many other minerals such as magnesium, copper, selenium and zinc play some role in cardiovascular health.

It is the opinion of this writer that the actual nutrient content of our foods has declined during the last 60 years or more due mostly to intensive farming practices including genetically modified organisms (GMO).

The challenge in all of this is that it is difficult to turn clues found in fieldwork into solid scientific research. For example, vitamins and minerals work in synergy therefore it is impossible to accurately assess their effects as separate elements. Vitamin A and D are needed for magnesium and calcium absorption, vitamin C works with vitamin E and vitamin E works with selenium.

There is also the physical insufficiency that more and more people are exhibiting such as in the digestive and endocrine system, which may inhibit nutrient absorption even if the food is high in nutritive value. Furthermore, the vitamin and nutrient content of our foods varies tremendously so we cannot rely on nutrient tables to determine the quantities of vitamin and mineral we are consuming.

Synthetic supplementation is not the answer and wouldn't be my choice of therapy as it can often times be counterproductive. For example, in the past vitamin D2 was added to milk, and was causing decalcification of the hard tissues and calcification of the soft tissues such as the arteries. For this reason, D2 was quietly dropped as an additive and replaced with D3. Synthetic D3 however, is showing that it is poorly absorbed. In general, vitamins from food work more efficiently, and are needed in smaller quantities, than synthetic vitamins.

We also have to look at the role that fats have in our diet. The Masai in Africa get 60 percent of their calories from fat and are free of heart disease. The original diet of the Eskimo and North American Indians contained up to 80 percent of calories from fat and there is no evidence that they suffered from heart disease. We now know that too much of omega-6 fatty acids and not enough omega-3 fatty acid may lead to blood clots, which can lead to heart attacks.

What I have observed in the field is that those who are trying to avoid eating too much fat often replace their fat calories with carbohydrate calories, which are usually in the form of refined flour or sugar. Yet several researchers have published studies that show a link between refined carbohydrates, especially sugar, and increased heart disease. Of course excess sugar consumption is also associated with increased incidence of diabetes, and diabetics can be prone to heart disease. Butter fat and coconut oil contain fatty acids that protect against viruses and pathogenic bacteria and enhance the immune system. Polynesians of not too distant past consumed coconut milk on a daily basis, but had no or low levels of heart disease.

Studies on the effects of vitamins and minerals with cardiovascular health must continue to be conducted with great care. Experts in the biochemistry of human nutrition should be involved in designing the studies, something that rarely occurs. The studies should be designed to include built-in protection against bias outcomes – from those that are strongly against the view that nutrition plays a role in heart disease. Of course there also must be some form of protection from those who want to capitalize on the supplement industries.

From a Hawaiian healing perspective, to maintain a healthy body is to build it from the bottom up. The foundation to health is to start with an appropriate colon cleansing program or supervised fast to suit your condition and needs. It is from this point that we can rapidly restore healing or to break the blueprint from disease. I have seen high blood pressure normalize after a period of fasting and a committed lifestyle change. High blood pressure is a tell tale sign that may indicate future heart disease. Dr. Al Wolfsen, a chiropractor/naturopath and friend of Auntie Margaret's (one of my teachers) told me of how he was able to immediately help a person who was having a heart attack using aggressive amounts of cayenne pepper (one teaspoon) in juice or water.

Another aspect to consider is the stress caused by our societal separation mentality, and the prolonged effects of loneliness, which may lead to heart problems. There are so many things to observe and to consider, but we should look into all possibilities.

So what can we do to protect ourselves against heart disease? Most of the guidelines out there today are pretty straightforward, although when considering these guidelines your individual makeup must be taken into account. Whatever you decide, if you are still afraid of saturated fats and cholesterol, you will find yourself in a continual struggle toward dietary health. Avoiding foods with saturated fat and cholesterol will not only deprive your body of essential nutrients, but the substituted foods you use will contain elements (polyunsaturated oils, trans fatty acids, refined flour and sugar) that have been associated with higher risks of heart disease.

Something to think about:

- Don't smoke.
- Exercise to your abilities and capabilities.
- Eat nutrient rich foods (live foods!) – organic fruits and vegetables.
- Don't overwork (find equal play time).
- Get out of polluted environment.
- Eat high quality meats (wild fish, grass fed animals, fats).
- Supplement diet with foods rich in protective factors (cod live oil, brewers yeast, flax oil, raw coconut oil, kelp).

- Do periodic supervised colon cleansing or supervised fasting programs.
- Live in a sustainable, supportive community.
- Educate yourself and take responsibility.

Mahalo.

60-Day Colon Cleansing Challenge

Indigenous Botanicals Support Group

Through his 30 plus years of clinical experiences, Dr. Maka'ala Yates, D.C. has found that cleansing the body on a regular basis is the basic foundation to being well. With enough information and by taking action, the average person can have a strong, healthy, functioning, youthful body and mind. The first step to feeling better is to cleanse the digestive tract (small and large intestines) and eliminate parasites from the body. Without this cleansing the body will be challenged in many ways including problems with absorption and assimilation. More importantly an abundance of toxins can accumulate that deteriorate the body's defense system and cause the body to function poorly.

The primary vision of Indigenous Botanicals™ is to help "bring the healer back into the family" by instilling independence through education. A wisdom centered knowledge that is based on ancient healing techniques that have worked for more than a 1000 years for the ancient Hawaiian people.

Our Hawaiian ancestors gave us tools to make it through the evolutionary changes they anticipated for generations to come---not only for the Hawaiian people, but also for all the people of the planet. The time has come for all of us to break the blueprint to disease and turn towards ourselves for healing, for remembering, and for our future.

We want to help people regain independence from health related problems, to break blueprints of lifestyle patterns that do not serve them anymore, and to re-establish self reliance by eliminating dependency on modern health care systems that do not work.

Despite the enormous sums of money spent on health care each year, the U.S. is one of the sickest nations in the world today. The reason can be attributed to the fact that now more than ever we are constantly exposed to chemicals, pesticides, food additives, heavy metals, GMO foods, and more importantly the decrease in the nutritional value of our diet. These elements can manifest in many kinds of symptoms and ailments including fatigue, weak immune system, hormonal dysfunction, infertility, skin problems, psychological disorders and cancer. The most powerful tool available to us in order to prevent, alleviate, and reverse many of these acute and chronic conditions is a solid internal cleansing or detoxification therapy program. Once the body is allowed to catch up, then a specific dietary life-style change should be followed.

The body uses the colon, skin, lungs, kidneys and other organs to eliminate toxins as quickly as possible. But if these systems are clogged, sluggish or overburdened, the toxins back up into the body and can cause headaches, loss of energy, fatigue and aches and pains. Years of improper elimination can lead to the most severe health problems.

Internal cleansing is a preventive means to assist the body in keeping its channels of elimination open and cleansed so they can perform their vital functions. The practice of cleansing has existed for thousands of years and has played a central role in the lives of millions of people throughout the world. Cleansing the body of built up toxins can promote health and prevent degenerative disease.

Maka'ala's Story

Growing up in Honaunau, Kona, Hawaii in the '50s and 60's, I saw a lot of the old Hawaiian ways of sustainable healthy living. One of the most essential ingredients necessary for this type of supportive community living (*ahupua'a*) is a medicine elder (*kahuna la'au lapa'au*). Every district and sub-district on the Big Island of Hawaii had a "go to" elder who had remedies and antidotes for most health emergencies. The job of these elders was to keep everyone healthy and for those that got injured or sick, to be able to mend and restore their imbalances.

In Kona, we had Auntie Margaret as our *kahuna la'au lapa'au*. In my 16 plus years studying with her, I have seen her mend injuries and restore health to people in situations that would be considered miracles by today's standards. She was not only treating people within our *ahupua'a* (district), but also people from all over the world. "The foundation to restoring and maintaining health is a solid fasting or cleansing program," said Auntie Margaret.

The first fast I ever did was in 1979 under Auntie Margaret's supervision. I was about 31 years old and I am sure toxic to the max, especially with two tours to Vietnam and a lifestyle of eating junk foods. In those military days I was exposed to so many different kinds of chemicals including Agent Orange and a host of unknown injections. Later in life I grew to appreciate the tools given to me for optimal cleansing and detoxing of the body. After the first fast, I started noticing things I never paid attention to before. I became more sensitive to my inner self and the environment around me, including people. I felt so good after the first fast that I did four more that year. It was during the third solo fast while in Honolulu that something incredible happened to me. After eliminating in the toilet bowl, I noticed something about 3 to 4 feet long that was tubular in shape. Stunned and alarmed, I immediately phoned Auntie Margaret. She explained that it was a lining of the large intestine that stays with us from the time of birth to protect the digestive tract while growing up. As we get older it is a good idea to eliminate this so we can freshen and renew the walls of our digestive system. Many people are not aware of this and the importance of eliminating this at some point in life.

Since 1979, I have done dozens of various types of fasting programs, but have always had best results with the Hawaiian approach. It's effective and user-friendly with unbelievable results. I look and feel younger, my energy level never lowers and my health is at an all time high. The 60-day colon-cleansing program is the result of years of research and experimentation using synergistic organic and wild-crafted herbs to obtain optimal positive outcomes.

What is the 60-day cleanse?

The 60-Day Colon Cleansing & Detox Program is based on traditional Hawaiian healing principles. This unique and effective program has been successfully used for over 30 years. It has helped thousands of people improve their health by giving them a strong foundation to work from. The herbal formulations used have been combined synergistically by hand and include organic and wild-crafted herbs. The herbs provide healing and nutritional support for your body as it goes through the detoxification process.

The program consists of drinking a seawater flush mixture using the sea salt blend formulated by Indigenous Botanicals™. This Hawaiian colon flush technique is done just three times in the course of the 60 days. The colon powder and parasite elimination tincture are taken once in the morning and once at night. Once or twice a week, a bath is taken using a specially formulated detox bath formula. If a bathtub is not available then a footbath is a good alternative. There is a daily 3-4 oz. early morning cocktail drink of the seawater formula to help alkalize the body and replenish minerals. It is encouraged to eat wisely with health in mind during the next 60 days. Guideline for what to eat during this program as well as other lifestyle changes are provided in the "Ideal Health Manual."

After completing the program expect to feel energized and transformed!

Contents the Colon Cleansing Challenge

- 1 – 20 ounce colon cleansing powder formula
- 2 – 2-ounce dropper bottle of parasite elimination tinctures
- 1 – 20 ounce container detoxification bath formula
- 1 – 8 ounce container Indigenous Botanicals™ sea salt
- 1 – Program Guide
- Cost = contact us at manaola@centurylink.net or manalomi.my@gmail.com or visit us at www.indigenousbotanicals.net.

Rules for the cleansing challenge

Step 1
Day 1 (start between 6 a.m. – 7 a.m.)
1. Seawater Flush
    *   Mix 1 level tablespoon (about 16 grams) sea salt with ½ gallon (about 1½ liters) spring water.
    *   Add 1 fresh squeezed lemon to mixture.
    *   Drink entire seawater mixture within the next hour or so.
    *   You are ready for step 2 once water has flushed through your system and you have eliminated as completely as possible.
    *   When the flush is complete, take a teaspoon of the colon cleansing formula with ½ dropper of the anti-parasite tincture in a small glass of juice (citrus or grape is best, but absolutely no apple juice). Repeat this in the evening at least 1 hour after evening meal.

Note: On day one you will have to wait until you have completely eliminated before taking the formula, which is usually around 9 a.m. for most people!

Step 2
Days 2 through 30
1. Seawater Cocktail: Taken daily upon rising each morning.
    *   Prepare 1 quart (about ¾ liter) of spring water with ½ tablespoon (1½ teaspoon) Indigenous Botanical™ natural sea salt blend. Store liquid in a glass container (no refrigeration necessary).
    *   Each morning upon waking, mix about 4 ounces of the seawater mixture with squeezed lemon to taste in a glass then drink.
2. Colon Formula: Take one teaspoon twice daily.
    *   Anytime after your morning cocktail and at least ½ hour before breakfast.
    *   In the evening at least one hour after your dinner.

- Shake the colon formula with 4 ounces of your favorite juice (half juice + half spring water), or almond milk, or soymilk, or rice milk, etc. and drink immediately!
- Note: do not use apple juice, as it tends to bloat the stomach.
3. Anti-parasite tincture: Take ½ dropper full (about 25 – 30 drops) twice daily.
    - It is ok to mix the anti-parasite tincture with the colon formula drink.
4. Detox Bath Formula
    Once or twice a week take a relaxing bath by adding 1 ounce of the Detox Bath formula to a warm tub of water. If a tub is not available then prepare a footbath in a bucket of warm water with 1 ounce of the Detox Bath formula.

Step 3
Days 31 through 60
- Repeat Steps 1 & 2

Step 4
Day 61
- Finish the program with a seawater flush as described in step 1.

For more information please feel free to contact us anytime.
manaola@centurylink.net or manalomi.my@gmail.com
U.S.A.

Feed Your Body Wisely

"If modern medicine saves lives, why are we as a nation so unhealthy?"

Lendon H. Smith, M.D.

Biochemical Individuality

Dr. Roger Williams, one of the great nutritional research pioneers, was the first to coin the term "Biochemical Individuality." This phrase expresses the fact that no two people are exactly alike in our disease susceptibilities; therefore, we do not have the same dietary needs. For example, an accountant who sits most of the day using his/her brain has different daily nutrient needs than those of a professional football player.

By making safe adjustments in our nutrient intake, we can start functioning normally, and, hopefully, when dealing with diseases, without using medications. We have created a generation totally dependent upon medical doctors and have lost any desire to take responsibility to control our diseases.

The following outline will give you some suggestions to solve a few simple signs and symptoms using supplements before they develop into a disease:

1. Scalp
   * Dandruff: Too much sugar. Need essential fatty acids, B-Complex (especially B6), selenium, and paraminobenzoic acid.
   * Thinning hair: On estrogen? B6, folate should help. Check for low thyroid and/or low stomach acid.
   * Lots of perspiration on head: Deficient in vitamin D.

2. Ears

   Heavy wax: Use essential fatty acid.

   - Cracks behind ears: B6 & zinc.
   - Fluid behind eardrums: Spilanthes, mullein or stone root (herbs).

3. Eyes

   - Dark circles under eyes: Food sensitivity (i.e., milk).
   - Dilated pupils in infants: Milk allergy.
   - Floaters: Use bioflavonoids, choline, inositol, vitamin K.
   - Cataract: Rule out blood sugar problem, Bioflavonoids, vitamin B2, A, C & magnesium should help.

4. Nose

   - Bleeding: Food sensitivity. Vitamin A, C, beta-carotene, bioflavonoids will help.

5. Face

   - Acne: Too much sugar, if over 25 years old usually food sensitivity or low B6; zinc essential fatty acids will help.

6. Tongue

   - Canker sores: Food allergy, chocolate, walnuts, stress and menses.
   - Pale color: Anemia.
   - Geography tongue: Low B-complex, food allergies.

7. Neck

   - Swollen glands behind ears: On the back usually from food allergies.
   - Swollen glands under corner of jaw: Tonsillar infection; also food sensitivities. Gargle with warm water and sea salt.

8. Nails

   - Brittle, chipping, soft, splitting: Low stomach acid, low iron, low calcium and magnesium; possible low thyroid.

- White spots: Zinc deficiency.
- Transverse ridges: for women a nutrient deficiency during menses.

9. Hands
   - Cracks at fingertips: low zinc.
   - Swollen joints-distal (farthest joint out): Osteoarthritis, B6, B3 may help; allergy, avoid nightshade plants (potato, eggplant).
   - Tender middle joints: rheumatoid; try B3.
   - Carpal tunnel syndrome: B6
   - Warts: Vitamin A, especially if frequent bronchitis and bumps on arm.

10. Breast
    - Nodular tender cysts: Stop caffeine, chocolate, cola; Take vitamin E, B6, essential fatty acids, magnesium.
    - Tender where rib meets sternum: B6

11. Abdomen
    - Smelly gas: low stomach acid, low pancreatic enzymes, lactose intolerance, or food sensitivity.

12. Feet and Legs
    - Knee swollen: Try niacinamide.
    - Osgood-Schlatter (approximately 13 years old): Selenium and vitamin E.
    - Dry skin, flaky: Essential fatty acids.
    - Pain on moderate pressure over skin: Calcium, niacinamide.
    - Varicose veins: Use fiber, vitamin E, magnesium, bioflavonoids.

By recognizing these symptoms early on and providing the nutrients needed some real prevention could be accomplished before it manifests into something serious.

The Calorie Misconception

"A health-supporting diet is unfamiliar to us because we are used to rich foods and because we have been overpowered by advertising from the food and health industries. But it is important for us to realize that what we enjoy eating and what we believe is correct nutrition for our bodies is solely a result of our previous conditioning and, therefore, it can and must be changed."

John A. McDougall, M.D.

Why does eating to satisfy our hunger make us overweight? The answer that best fits is that our stomachs are not conducive to the high-calorie foods typically consumed by developed societies. The stomach does much better with a diet of starches, which are considered low-calorie foods. The myth that starches are fattening is far from the truth, but people will literally push the potatoes or rice away in order to lose weight. In developed countries, people are overweight because they eat too little starch and consume mostly high-calorie fats and oils in the form of meat, milk, cheese, nuts, seeds and vegetable oils. In the western societies, we would dramatically improve our health by eliminating the misconception that starches are fattening.

A brief overview of a calorie chart will help us understand why staying thin isn't such a difficult task. An average adult male who is active burns about 3,000 calories per day. One cup of cooked rice (about 150 grams) contains 178 calories, which means there are only about 1.2 calories per gram of rice. Beef has about 3.9 calories per gram and cheese has 4.0 calories per gram. The ideal food to have rapid weight loss is the potato, which has 0.6 calories per gram or about 85 calories per potato.

Foods are composed of five major ingredients:

1. Fats, 9 calories per gram
2. Proteins, 4 calories per gram

3. Carbohydrates (CHO), 4 calories per gram
4. Water, o calories per gram
5. Fiber, o calories per gram

The total calorie uptake will depend on the proportions of these five foods. For example, potatoes are primarily CHO consisting of 4 calories per gram, 0 calories per gram of fiber and 0 calories per gram of water with a total 0.6 calories per gram concentration.

The tendency is to eat too many calories before our stomachs are full and our hunger is satisfied from all the meat, dairy, nuts and seeds we eat. With starches, vegetables, and fruits our stomachs are full faster but filled with fewer calories. Also, foods low in calorie concentration take longer to eat therefore giving the brain time to receive information from the stomach that fullness has been reached.

Satisfaction of hunger occurs primarily by filling the stomach. Those foods with a low concentration of calories will fill our stomachs without providing excess calories. Contentment also comes from the slow absorption of food, which is best accomplished by complex CHO foods that are high in fiber.

An ideal health-supporting diet is simple to understand and put together. Any variety of starch makes up the main or largest portion of the meal, and the vegetables and fruit are added in smaller amounts to complement the starch main course. Generally speaking, the plant kingdom consists of starches, vegetables, and fruits.

Starches

Starches will be defined as foods that contain adequate amounts of readily available calories in the form of starch molecules. These molecules are made up of long chains of sugars, which are the basic unit of the body's energy supply. Starches should be supported by the right amounts of protein, essential fat, fiber, water, vitamins, and minerals. Starches should be your primary daily source of calories.

Fruits

Most of the sugars in fruits are in the form of sucrose, glucose, or fructose and therefore taste sweet. They are usually high in calories, fiber and vitamins. Most have protein, minerals, and essential fat that make it a nutritionally complete food. It is recommended that you keep the intake of fruits to a minimum due to their high content of simple sugars and easily available calories.

The combinations of starches, vegetables, and fruits provide an unlimited variety of meals for you to enjoy. The primary function of food is to supply calories to provide energy for our daily activities. Complex carbohydrates found in starches, vegetables, and fruits offer the most efficient and safest source of calories. These foods naturally have the nutritional components that support our innate healing processes and maintain our health. They contain the necessary protein (amino acids), essential fat, fiber, vitamins, minerals, and other nutrients to enable us to function at our fullest. Having a properly planned diet of these foods avoids excesses of cholesterol, fat, protein, simple sugar, salt, and environmental pollutants that can cause our health to fail.

Alkaline and Acid Forming Foods
A brief overview

The ideal pH for human blood is between 7.35 – 7.45, which is slightly alkaline. Anything above or below this range leads to ill health or disease. The biochemical term, pH, stands for potential of Hydrogen and it is a ratio measurement for acid to alkaline. Maintaining homeostasis (balanced pH) in the body is critical for long-term health.

In my many years helping people with minor illness or dis-ease, I have found that the average person's diet is overly acidic. An accumulation of acidity in the body develops into what is known as acidosis. Acidosis leads to many health problems. A balanced pH solves them.

German physiologist, Professor Otto Heinrich Warburg, won the Nobel Prize in 1931 for his "discovery of the nature and mode of action of the respiratory enzyme." Warburg firmly believed that there was a direct relationship between pH and oxygen. He reported that cancer cells maintain a lower pH, as low as 6.0, due to lactic acid production and elevated CO_2 (carbon dioxide). Higher pH means higher concentration of oxygen molecules, while lower pH means lower concentration of oxygen. The bottom line is that cancer cells will not grow in an oxygen rich environment and one with a balanced pH.

An acidic pH can occur from, an acid forming diet, emotional stress, toxic overload (internal or environmental), and/or immune reactions (oxygen and nutrient deprivation to cells). An accumulation of acids in the cell will occur when the body is not able to compensate for increase acidity due to lack of alkaline minerals in the body.

An acid-rich body will decrease the body's ability to absorb minerals and other nutrients, decrease energy production in the cells, decrease its ability to repair damaged cells, decrease its ability to detoxify heavy metals and other toxins, increase body fatigue and illness, and will encourage tumor cells to thrive.

One of the best things we can do to correct an overly acid body is to clean up our diet and lifestyle. For example, cut back on animal products that produce acidity like meat, eggs, and dairy and include more fresh fruits and vegetables. Also, decrease or eliminate processed foods like white flour, sugar, coffee and soft drinks. Recreational and pharmaceutical drugs are also acid forming as are artificial sweeteners.

A good rule of thumb to maintain optimal health is to have about 60% alkaline forming food and 40% acid forming food in your diet. If restoration of health is your quest then 80%/20% alkaline/acid forming food should be maintained.

In general, alkaline forming foods include: most fruits, green vegetables, peas, beans, lentils, seeds, nuts, and spices. Acid forming foods include: meat, fish, poultry, eggs, grains and legumes.

The chart below is intended only as a general guideline to alkaline and acid forming foods:

Alkalizing Foods

Alfalfa	Barley Grass	Beet Greens
Beets	Broccoli	Cabbage
Carrot	Cauliflower	Celery
Chard Greens	Chlorella	Collard Greens
Cucumber	Dandelions	Dulce
Edible Flowers	Eggplant	Fermented Veggies
Garlic	Green Beans	Green Peas
Kale	Kohlrabi	Lettuce
Mushrooms	Mustard Greens	Nightshade Veggies
Onions	Parsnips (high glycemic)	Peas
Peppers	Pumpkin	Radishes
Rutabaga	Sea Veggies	Spinach, green
Spirulina	Sprouts	Sweet Potatoes
Tomatoes	Watercress	Wheat Grass
Daikon	Dandelion Root	Kombu
Maitake	Nori	Reishi
Shitake	Umeboshi	Wakame
Apricot	Avocado	Banana (high glycemic)
Berries	Blackberries	Cantaloupe
Cherries, sour	Coconut, fresh	Currants
Dates, dried	Figs, dried	Grapes
Grapefruit	Honeydew Melon	Lemon
Lime	Muskmelons	Nectarine
Orange	Peach	Pear
Pineapple	Raisins	Raspberries
Rhubarb	Strawberries	Tangerine
Tomato	Tropical Fruits	Umeboshi Plums
Watermelon	Chestnuts	Millet
Almonds	Tofu (fermented)	Whey Protein Powder
Tempeh (fermented)	Curry	Chili Pepper

Cinnamon	Miso	Ginger
Herbs (all)	Tamari	Mustard
Sea Salt	Water	Mustard
Bee Pollen	Fresh Fruit Juice	Apple Cider Vinegar
Lecithin Granules	Mineral Water	Green Juices
Probiotic Cultures	Soured Dairy Products	Molasses, blackstrap
Veggie Juices		

Acidifying Foods

Corn	Lentils	Olives
Winter Squash	Blueberries	Canned or Glazed Fruits
Cranberries	Currants	Plums**
Prunes**	Amaranth	Barley
Bran, oat	Bran, wheat	Bread
Corn	Cornstarch	Crackers, soda
Flour, wheat	Flour, white	Hemp Seed Flour
Kamut	Macaroni	Noodles
Oatmeal	Oats (rolled)	Quinoa
Rice (all)	Rice Cakes	Rye
Spaghetti	Spelt	Wheat Germ
Wheat	Almond Milk	Black Beans
Chick Peas	Green Peas	Kidney Beans
Lentils	Pinto Beans	Red Beans
Rice Milk	Soy Beans	Soy Milk
White Beans	Butter	Cheese
Cheese, Processed	Ice Cream	Ice Milk
Cashews	Legumes	Peanut Butter
Peanuts	Pecans	Tahini
Walnuts	Bacon	Beef
Carp	Clams	Cod
Corned Beef	Fish	Haddock
Lamb	Lobster	Mussels
Organ Meats	Oyster	Pike
Pork	Rabbit	Salmon
Sardines	Sausage	Scallops
Shellfish	Shrimp	Tuna
Turkey	Veal	Venison
Avocado Oil	Butter	Canola Oil
Corn Oil	Flax Oil	Hemp Seed Oil

Lard	Olive Oil	Safflower Oil
Sesame Oil	Sunflower Oil	Carob
Corn Syrup	Sugar	Beer
Hard Liquor	Spirits	Wine
Catsup	Cocoa	Coffee
Mustard	Pepper	Soft Drinks
Vinegar	Aspirin	Chemicals
Drugs, Medicinal	Drugs, Psychedelic	Herbicides
Pesticides	Tobacco	Beer: pH 2.5
Coca-Cola: pH 2	Coffee: pH 4	

A final note, be smart by eating and living smart. Eat as cleanly and healthily as possible. This means, don't eat processed or fast foods, chemically laden or nutrient deficient foods. You should also understand what foods are alkaline and what are acidic. I am not saying to give up on eating meat or never to drink a beer or a glass of wine, however, moderation is important. Your vegetable portion should definitely be larger than your meat portion. Eat organic when possible and grow you own garden when possible. Eating properly is the fundamental basis for restoring your body's pH to homeostasis.

Green Drink

A Green Drink is frequently suggested as a means to rapidly flush the liver of toxins and to assist in activating the pancreas. It is soothing to the bowel and the chlorophyll is a natural painkiller. Although we commonly use this drink as a morning breakfast to boost the energy level it is highly recommended for the overall detoxification process on a cellular level. A Green Drink is usually made from the following:

Any Edible Green Leaf	Endive	Fresh Green Okra	Beets
Carrots	Bell Peppers*	Escarole	BeetTops
Radishes*	Lettuce	Celery	Cauliflower
Cucumber	Aloes	Mint	Romaine
Green Beans	Leeks, Onions*	OnionTops	
Spinach	Garden Pea Leaves	Cabbage*	
Nasturtium seeds	Broccoli*	Collards*	

* These vegetables may cause excessive gas in some persons.

You may add the following to the green drink for flavor:

Yogurt	Apple juice	Pineapple juice	Honey
V-8 juice	Fresh apple (1/qt.)	Tomato juice	
Lemon water	Comfrey leaf	Grape juice (unsweetened)	

The best method of preparing a green drink is with an auger system juicer. If you do not have a juicer you can use a blender. Place the greens you are going to use in the blender and add a small amount of distilled water. Run the blender at puree speed until you have pulped the vegetables. Place a clean linen cloth over a bowl and pour the pulp into the linen. Draw the linen up to make a bag and then twist the bag until you've forced as much juice as possible into the bowl. Measure out the needed amount. Add flavoring if you desire and drink immediately. Green drinks do not store well since they rapidly undergo lacto-fermentation and lose their effectiveness. Therefore, a green drink must be made up fresh each day.

In the absence of either a juicer or a blender you can purchase chlorophyll extract from a health food store. It is not as energizing as chlorophyll extracted from fresh greens but it will still help. Mix one tablespoon to three ounces water. It tastes a little grassy so you might want to mix it in some other vegetable juice to disguise the taste if it's unpleasant to you.

A good green drink powder mix in a morning smoothie will also boost your energy & vitality level. You can the following ingredients to boost your health:

Spirulina – An aqua cultivated food with approximately 65% Protein that is 95% digestible (most meat protein has only 20% digestibility). Spirulina is low in calories (3.6 calories per gram), yet it is the highest whole food source of Vitamin B12. It is high in betacarotene (25 times higher that carrots) and richer in chlorophyll than wheat grass or alfalfa.

Chlorella – Often called the "Emerald Food," this algae contains over 50% protein that is approximately 79% digestible due to a special process that breaks the cell wall. Chlorella is a rich source of essential natural vitamins and minerals.

Barley and Wheat Grass Juice – Harvested from young cereal plants that are cut, carefully juiced and dried into a green powder. Both are rich sources of Chlorophyll and human blood (hemoglobin) is similar in nature, an observation that gives credence to Barley and Wheat Grass as two "Green Super foods."

Icelandic Kelp and Nova Scotia dulse are rich in minerals and protein. Kelp is known for its iodine content, while dulse is red in color and is noted for its rich minerals and naturally occurring lithium.

Why Our Body Needs Adequate Water

"In health and in sickness, pure water is one of heaven's choicest blessings. Its proper use promotes health. It is the beverage, which God provided to quench the thirst of animals and humans. Drunk freely, it helps to supply the necessities of the system and assists nature to resist disease."
Ellen G. White, *The Ministry of Healing, p.237*

You may have heard that everyone should drink eight cups of water a day, but do you know why? The answer is to maintain the body's proper water balance. Water is essential to life; it is present in all living body cells. If the body is to function properly, the body's daily output of water must be replenished. Research has shown that, for adults, approximately eight cups of water are needed to maintain this healthful water balance.

Water helps in the digestive process to break up, soften and transport food particles from stomach to intestines. Then the body's blood, which is 90 percent water, circulates nutrients. Water controls body temperature through perspiration, which occurs to some degree even when one is not aware of it. Each day the skin of even a sedentary person loses moisture equal to about two cups of water.

Water is a lubricant preventing friction between the body's joints and muscles, the same way oil prevents friction between machinery parts. During manual labor and many strenuous sports, the body is stretched, twisted, and bent in ways that wouldn't be possible if water weren't present.

Water reduces stress on the circulatory system during sports activities, and it helps the blood carry energy providing carbohydrates to the body's cells. During illness, greater water intake helps regulate body temperature and control fever. By using water for all its functions and losing water through perspiration and breathing, the body uses an average of three quarts each day. Most people consume approximately one quart in their daily diet, so where does the rest come from? By drinking at least eight cups of water. Your urine should be pale if your water intake is adequate.

CAYENNE: *Healing with Heat*

Cayenne peppers belong to the species Capsicum annuum. There are about 20 species and hundreds of varieties in the genus Capsicum, indigenous to tropical America. In their native habitat, they are perennial and woody, growing to seven feet tall, though in American gardens they are grown as annuals, reaching a height of about three feet. Capsicum is believed to have originated in an area of southern Brazil and Bolivia, from which it spread to various parts of South and Central America.

In the 1970's, Dr. John Christopher popularized cayenne. He wrote in his School of Natural Healing, "This herb is a great food for the circulatory system in that it feeds the necessary elements into the cell structure of the arteries, veins and capillaries so that these regain the elasticity of youth again, and the blood pressure adjusts itself to normal."

Capsicum is also a powerful local stimulant, which quickens, stirs up, excites, and increases nervous sensibility. It gives stimulus to functional activity and energy in the body. It increases the power of the pulse and carries the blood to all parts of the body, tending to equalize and restore the balance of circulation in all parts.

Cayenne is a medicinal and nutritional herb – it is the number one stimulant – the purest and most certain stimulant of the medicinal herbs (according to Potter's Cyclopaedia) and is a very powerful nutritive food.

Cayenne stimulates and increases the blood flow, which gets the blood and the healing nutrients and chemicals to where they are needed most. There is no other herb that moves the blood faster to the head and brain than cayenne. Getting more blood to the brain can have great positive effects on stress, vision, thinking, and memory. This may also be the first step in healing a brain injury or disease. It will also keep anyone from fainting or losing consciousness.

Cayenne is most effective for heart and blood circulation problems, and for angina pectoris, palpitations, and cardiac arrhythmias. It's a miracle for congestive heart failure. It is specific for anyone who has any type of circulatory problems, such as high or low blood pressure, elevated cholesterol, triglycerides and fats, even varicose veins.

With the heart, cayenne is great for prevention as well as for the treatment of disease. It relieves the pain of angina pectoris by helping to get more blood to the heart muscle itself. And, if a person has a heart attack, cayenne is the surest first aid remedy.

Cayenne is listed in the Merck Index as an official carminative and stomach stimulant. If a person's digestive problems are due to a lack of digestive strength, digestive juices, or stagnation in the stomach, cayenne is a godsend. It stops the bleeding of stomach and duodenal ulcers. It also increases better circulation in the stomach wall, which speeds up the healing process.

Cayenne also stimulates your pancreas to release more hydrochloric acid, enzymes, and even promotes your liver and gall bladder to release more bile. All of these actions increase your digestion. For digestive problems, a little cayenne can go a long way. It is best to begin with a small amount, like 1/8 teaspoon, eight times a day, and increase slowly as you feel better. It can also be added to aloe, slippery elm bark and licorice root, to buffer it, if desired as all of these additional herbs also heal the stomach lining.

Remember, what determines the potency of cayenne is not the name it's called but the intensity of its heat, which is determined by the quantity of the potent chemicals in cayenne, capsaicin, and its resins. The more of these chemicals that are in cayenne, the hotter it is and also the stronger and more effective it is in healing.

The heat is measured in heat units, incorrectly called BTUs (British Thermal Units) but correctly called Scoville Units, or just heat units.

All capsicum is rated between 0 and 300,000 heat units. Paprika has no heat and is rated 0 heat units. Most actual cayenne peppers are rated between 30,000 and 80,000. Jalapeno peppers are between 50,000 and 80,000. Serrano peppers are at about 100,000. African bird peppers are about 200,000 and Mexican habaneros are between 250,000 and 300,000.

Activated Charcoal

Charcoal has been used effectively in the healing arts for centuries. Doctors still use it today as a healing agent, an antidote for poisons, and an effective treatment for indigestion and gas. Modern industry also relies on charcoal to deodorize, decolorize and purify solutions. Charcoal can do these varied tasks because of its amazing ability to attract other substances to its surface and hold them there. This is called adsorption. Charcoal can adsorb thousands of times its own weight in gases, heavy metals, poisons, and other chemicals, thus making them ineffective or harmless.

The form of charcoal used in modern medical science is Activated Charcoal USP, a pure naturally produced, wood charcoal carbon that has no carcinogenic properties. Activated charcoal is an odorless, tasteless powder. One teaspoonful of it has a surface area of more than 10,000 square feet. This unique feature allows it to adsorb large amounts of chemicals or poisons. The powder must be stored in a tightly sealed container, as it readily adsorbs impurities from the atmosphere. Charcoal from burnt toast is not effective, and charcoal briquettes can be dangerous because they contain fillers and petrochemicals to help them ignite.

Scientific experiments over many years attest to the effectiveness of charcoal as an antidote. In one experiment, 100 times the lethal dose of Cobra venom was mixed with charcoal and injected into a laboratory animal. The animal was not harmed. In other experiments, arsenic and strychnine were mixed with charcoal and ingested by humans under laboratory conditions. The subjects survived even though the poison dosages were 5 to 10 times the lethal dose.

Home Use Of Activated Charcoal

Indigestion and Gas

A study made in 1981 shows that activated charcoals cuts down on the amount of gas produced by beans and other gas-producing foods It adsorbs the excess gas as well as the bacteria that from the gas. Activated charcoal helps to eliminate bad breath, because it cleanses both the mouth and the digestive tract. It is also helpful in relieving symptoms of nervous diarrhea, traveler's diarrhea (Turista), spastic colon, indigestion, and peptic ulcers. For such problems take between 1 teaspoon and 1½ tablespoons of powdered charcoal up to 3 times a day. Take it between meals, as food can reduce its effectiveness. Swirl the charcoal in a glass of water and drink it down or mix it with olive oil for easy ingestion by using a spoon.

Activated charcoal is inexpensive, simple to use and is a time-tested natural remedy that has many valuable uses without dangerous side effects or contradictions, a very efficient cleaner of the body when taken orally. It also helps to purify the blood.

Charcoal may adsorb and inactivate other medications. Usually you can take charcoal two hours before or after other drugs. If you are taking prescription drugs, check with your doctor before beginning treatment with charcoal. You can take charcoal intermittently for long periods or regularly for up to 12 weeks. However, do not take it regularly for long periods.

Treatment of Wounds, Ulcers, and Bruises

Lancet, the prestigious British medical journal, describes the use of charcoal compresses to speed the healing of wounds, and eliminate their odors. This article tells about the amazing ability of human skin to allow transfer through its permeable membrane and pores, of liquids, gasses and even micro-particles by the application of moist activated charcoal compresses and poultices, which actually draw bacteria and poisons through the skin and into the poultice or compress. Poultices must be kept moist and warm to allow this healing process to take place.

Make a poultice by putting 1- 2 tablespoons of charcoal powder in a container and adding just enough water to make a paste. Spread the paste on a paper towel, cloth, or piece of gauze cut to fit the area to be treated. Make sure the cloth is moist, warm, and thoroughly saturated with the paste. Place it over the wound cloth-side down and cover it with a piece of plastic wrap or plastic bag cut to overlap the poultice by an inch on every side. Fix in place with adhesive tape. Poultices should be changed every 6-10 hours. Do not put charcoal directly on broken skin, as it may cause a tattooing effect.

Goat Whey

Goat Whey is high in sodium & potassium not to mention many other minerals. Stomach disorders (chronic indigestion, intestinal irritation, constipation, ulcers) as well as joint problems (arthritis, osteoporosis) are often signs that bioorganic sodium (food sodium) is deficient in the body. Sodium is primarily stored in the walls of the stomach and small intestine (joints too).

This makes the tissues of the stomach very alkaline, which is needed to withstand the hydrochloric acid normally produced in the stomach. Without sodium the acid in these tissues would destroy walls of the stomach.

Whenever acids are produced anyplace in the body through devitalized foods, mental strain and stress, sodium is taken from the stomach and other storage areas to neutralize them. With this imbalance digestion is impaired and we know that there are many health problems from improperly digested foods. The stomach, intestines, joint and ligaments are sodium organs and are in constant need of sodium in solution (food sodium).

Bioorganic potassium (food potassium) deficiency may cause heart irregularity, fatigue and immune system problems. It is mainly stored in the muscle, including the heart muscle, neutralizing acid wastes in the muscle tissue and controlling the acid alkaline balance together with sodium.

Potassium does many of the same things sodium does, which is why they are almost always found together in the body. One of the most important metabolic functions our bodies perform is to maintain a specific pH. The acid alkaline balance in the body is kept nearly constant by the electrolytes (mainly sodium and potassium). So if we are walking around with an imbalance for whatever reason one of the best foods to help our bodies "catch up" is Goat Whey.

Uses: About 1 teaspoon of goat whey in the morning in a smoothie, or juice will assist the digestive system to function at an optimal level. This will help eliminate bloating, especially after meals, difficulty assimilating or digesting foods (a condition that is more common in the U.S. than led to believe) & gas.

Enzymes for a healthy body

Enzymes are vitally important for all the functions of your body. They are considered the "spark of life" and without them you couldn't digest or absorb food for example. We would die without enzymes. Enzymes run your entire body.

Enzymes are protein molecules that carry a vital energy factor needed for every chemical action and reaction that occurs in our bodies. Approximately 2,700 different enzymes are found in the human body. Enzymes combined with coenzymes (vitamins and minerals) form at least one hundred thousand various chemicals that help us to hear, see, feel, move, digest food, and think. Every organ, tissue and all the one hundred trillion cells in our body depend upon the reaction of enzymes and their energy factor. Nutrition cannot be explained without describing the vital role played by enzymes.

One of the first steps to improving enzyme deficiencies in your body is to chew your food well. Including raw foods in your diet is another step for improving enzymatic activity. Unfortunately, most people who follow a western diet, virtually starve their bodies of enzymes by eating too much of processed or overcooked foods.

When food is heated at a sustained temperature of more than 120 degrees, all enzymes are destroyed. Enzymes in saliva help the cause, but most people don't chew their food well enough to properly start off the digestive process. So most of the food we eat reaches the stomach without the benefit of enzymes, which means it's not properly pre-digested.

To compensate for the lack of pre-digestion, stomach acids are over-produced, which can cause heartburn or acid reflux. As much as the stomach is doing its best efforts, food that's still not properly digested reaches the small intestine. This puts a large amount of stress on the pancreas and the endocrine system in general to provide reserves of enzymes. When this stress is repeated day after day, the pancreas suffers.

Recent studies have shown that virtually 100% of people on the typical 'western' diet have an enlarged pancreas by the time they are 40.

If you happen to be one of those who follow a western dietary lifestyle and want to speed up the recovery, there is something I came across a few years ago that may help. Seaprose-S (Protease S is another name used) is a specific type of enzyme (known as proteolytic or protease) that breaks down proteins and regulates their functions. This enzyme is a key to several important tasks, including the reduction of inflammation and the elimination of mucous. Studies have shown that it may also be a natural antibiotic, capable of neutralizing dangerous bacteria like streptococcus. This proteolytic enzyme is a semi-alkaline serine-proteinase produced by the fungus Aspergillus melleus.

Nature has placed enzymes in food to help us digest everything we eat – starches, fat, protein, and fiber, instead of forcing the enzymes secreted in our bodies to do all of the work. A diet high in raw fruits and vegetables contain high amounts of "active" enzymes. The more enzymes you get, the healthier you are. When we eat overcooked or processed foods, we are eating dead or denatured foods. Dead foods have no living enzymes and most of its nutrients are diminished significantly.

The seven categories of food enzymes:

1. Lipase – breakdown fat
2. Protease – breakdown protein
3. Cellulase – breakdown fiber
4. Amyase – breakdown starch
5. Lactase – breakdown dairy foods
6. Sucrase – breakdown sugars
7. Maltase – breakdown grains

As we get older (30 – 35), there is a definite decline in the level of digestive enzymes (an established medical fact) produced in the stomach, pancreas and small intestine.

Unfortunately, a lot of our raw foods today carry very low amounts of enzymes due to overcooking, chemical preservatives, irradiation, and other processing and preservative methods. The results are that much of our foods (even nutritional supplements) that we eat are passed through and out of our bodies not fully digested therefore not fully assimilated by our bodies.

The source of most health problems can be linked directly to improperly digested foods. When food remains undigested in the colon for over six hours, it begins to putrefy, which results in high levels of toxins and poisonous waste. These toxins and poisons are then circulated back into the blood stream (autointoxication), which delivers these toxins to every organ in the body.

Enzyme Deficiencies

1. Protease
    - Creates alkaline excess in the blood.
    - Leads to hypoglycemia – mood swings and irritability.
    - Compromise immune system.
    - Chronic ear infection and fluid in the ears.
2. Lipase
    - High cholesterol, high triglycerides, difficulty losing weight and tendency towards diabetes.

Daily supply of enzymes (from food source although supplements can help the body catch up) can help specific conditions:

- Premature aging, arthritis, and other inflammatory conditions; cancer; cardiovascular diseases; circulatory problems; gynecological problems; herpes; injuries; multiple sclerosis; skin problems; lupus erythematous and other autoimmune diseases; viruses and weight problems.

MY Favorite Recipes
Random listings

Miso Salad Dressing

This recipe requires your own amount of each ingredient according to your taste.

- ¼ cup extra virgin olive oil
- ¼ cup water
- ¼ cup brown rice miso
- 1½ tablespoons brown rice vinegar
- 1 heaping tablespoon chopped onion
- Avocado
- Carrots (small or half)
- 1 tablespoon sesame seeds
- ½ teaspoon sesame oil
- 1 garlic (clove)
- 2 tablespoons honey or rice malt
- Herbs & spices to taste (spike, soy sauce or gomasio)

Place all ingredients in a blender and blend until smooth. Sometimes I add a few sprigs of fresh dill before blending.

Teriyaki Sauce

- 1 cup tamari (I usually dilute this with equal or less amount of water)
- 2 cloves garlic grated
- 3 pieces of ginger grated
- 1 teaspoon honey
- ¼ teaspoon sesame oil (use sparingly)
- 1 teaspoon sesame seeds

Gobo with Garlic

- 3 or 4 burdock roots (fresh)
- 5 cloves fresh garlic (minced)

- 1/3 cup (or less) rice vinegar
- ½ cup (or less) olive oil
- Tamari to taste

Select un-withered roots. Wash with a stiff brush and trim ends. Chop into small uniform pieces (julienne is ok). Steam for about 30 – 40 minutes until tender. While hot, add garlic, olive oil, rice vinegar and tamari. Mix well and let set until room temperature or cool. Adjust for taste and enjoy.

Sweet and Sour Tempeh

Steam tempeh for about 20 minutes then marinate in tamari and ginger. Set aside the tempeh then sauté onions, peppers (red & yellow ones are great), carrots and garlic in olive oil. Add pineapple and sauce (pineapple juice, arrowroot and cider vinegar) and the tempeh. Let simmer for a few minutes then serve over basmati or brown rice.

Gomasio

Japanese sesame/seaweed seasoning
- 1 cup brown (un-hulled) sesame seeds
- ½ tablespoon or less sea salt
- 1 average strip kombu seaweed

Using a dry cast iron skillet on medium heat, lightly toast the sea salt and kombu seaweed. Take out the kombu and break into smaller pieces and return to the skillet. Add the sesame seeds to the kombu and sea salt and toast for an additional 5 – 10 minutes. Don't burn the sesame seeds (golden color is good). Take off the burner and allow the mixture to cool to room temperature. Grind the seeds to about cornmeal consistency or to your liking. Store in airtight container and don't refrigerate. Use within a month or two.

Basic Chutney

- 4 cups diced fruit (blended or single). My favorite is mango.
- 1 teaspoon cumin seeds

- 1 teaspoon anise seeds
- 1 teaspoon crushed chili peppers
- ¼ cup or more brown sugar
- 1 pinch sea salt to taste
- ½ teaspoon clove & nutmeg depending of flavor
- 3 tablespoon cold press olive oil
- Heat oil in pan
- Add cumin and anise seeds.
- When the mix starts to brown, add chilies, wait a short while then add fruit and stir.
- Add salt, sugar, and clove/nutmeg and cook until nice and glossy.

Seal in a cleaned or sterile jar.

Kimchi (kimchee)
- 1 Napa cabbage
- ½ cup sea salt
- 8 ounces daikon radish, peeled and cut into 2-inch matchsticks
- 4 medium scallions, ends trimmed, cut into 1-inch pieces (use all parts)
- 1/3 cup Korean red pepper powder or other chili powder
- 1/4 cup peeled and minced fresh ginger (from about a 2-ounce piece)
- 1 tablespoon minced garlic cloves (from 6 to 8 medium cloves)

Chop into bite size pieces, Napa cabbage (or won bok), broccoli, carrots and optional cucumber. Sprinkle sea salt and mix well with hands. Add enough cool water to cover vegies and cover with plastic wrap then let sit at room temperature for at least 12 hours or overnight.

Drain in a colander and rinse in cool filtered water. Gently squeeze excess liquid out of cabbage and transfer to medium bowl. Place the remaining ingredients in a separate bowl and mix thoroughly then add the vegies. Pack in a clean jar that can be sealed. Let this sit in a cool, dark place for 24 hours (the mixture may bubble). Open the jar to let the gases escape, then reseal and refrigerate at least 48 hours before eating (kimchi is best after fermenting about 1 week). Refrigerate for up to 1 month.

Pilaf Mélange
This is a combination of quinoa, corn, squash and tofu.

- 2 cups fresh corn (cut from cobs)
- 2 cups acorn or other squash (cut into small pieces equal to the corn)
- 2 cups carrot (cut like the squash)
- 2 cups tofu cut into small squares
- 1 tablespoon sunflower oil
- 1 teaspoon (tsp.) turmeric
- 1 tsp. cumin
- 1 tsp. coriander
- 1 tsp. fennel
- 1 garlic (clove) or more to taste
- 2 cups quinoa (rinsed)
- 7 cups water

Lightly sauté the garlic in oil then add the spices. Add the vegies and tofu and sauté lightly. Add the quinoa and sauté for another minute or two stirring constantly. Add the water, cover and simmer for 15 – 20 minutes. Let the mixture sit 10 or more minutes, covered. Serve when ready.

Spiced Milk
- 1 cup raw milk (almond is my favorite)
- ½ teaspoon (tsp.) honey
- ½ tsp. turmeric
- ½ tsp. ginger
- ¼ tsp. cumin

Blend above ingredients and heat. Enjoy.

Eggplant with Caprese Salsa

For the eggplant
- 2 pounds of eggplant trimmed and cut into ¼ inch thick rounds
- 2 tablespoons sea salt grounded coarsely
- 3 tablespoons extra virgin olive oil
- 2 teaspoons dried oregano
- ½ teaspoon ground black pepper
- ½ teaspoon hot red pepper flakes
- 3 cloves garlic, minced
- 3 tablespoons chopped fresh flat leaf parsley

For the salsa
- 1 large ripe tomato, diced
- 8 basil leaves, slivered, sprigs for garnish
- 2 tablespoons extra virgin olive oil
- 1 (5 ounce) chunk fresh mozzarella cheese, diced
- 2 tablespoons fresh lemon juice
- Coarse sea salt and freshly ground black pepper

First step, place eggplant rounds in single layers on a large baking sheet. Sprinkle both sides with salt; let rest for about 30 minutes. Preheat grill to medium.

Second step, rinse eggplant slices under cold filtered water and blot dry on both sides with paper towel. Rub oil on both sides of eggplant and sprinkle with oregano, black pepper, pepper flakes, garlic, and parsley.

Third step, arrange eggplant slices on grill and cook until browned on both sides (5 – 8 minutes per side). Work the eggplant around so it doesn't get burnt. Transfer to a platter and keep warm with tin foil.

Fourth step, to make the salsa, combine tomato, mozzarella, basil, oil, and lemon juice and mix well. Add salt and pepper to taste and let rest for 5 minutes. Spoon salsa over slices of eggplant and garnish with basil sprigs. As an option, put readied eggplant rounds on slices of crusty bread – brushed with olive oil and grilled. Yummy.

Dolly's Famous Pumpkin Pie

This is my mother's award winning pumpkin pie recipe and my favorite. I love you mom!

Preheat oven to 400 degrees
- 2 eggs slightly beaten
- 1¾ cups steamed pumpkin or sweet meat squash
- ¼ cup brown sugar or less amount of honey
- ½ teaspoon salt
- 2 teaspoons pumpkin pie spice
- 1½ cups milk (I like homemade raw almond milk)

After 15 min. turn heat down to 350 degrees for 30 minutes or until cooked

Drop Scones
- 2 cups whole wheat pastry flour or other flour
- 1 tablespoon baking powder
- Pinch of ground sea salt
- ¼ cup cold butter (raw is best), cut into small pieces
- 2 eggs beaten
- ½ cup milk
- Optional fruit (banana, mangoes, and papaya are my favorites)

Preheat oven to 400 degrees.
Mix flour, baking powder, sugar, salt, butter together. Using two knives, cut in flour mixture, and then mix briefly with a fork until dough looks like corn meal. In a separate bowl, combine eggs and milk and beat together. Pour egg mixture into flour mixture and blend until dry ingredients are just moistened. Add fresh fruit of your choice as an option. Drop spoonful batter (3-ounce rounds or smaller) onto a well-greased cookie pan. An ice cream scoop works well. Bake until tops are golden brown (about 18 – 20 minutes).

Macadamia and Coconut Crusted Chicken

- 1 cup almond meal
- 1 cup coconut milk
- 1 cup finely chopped roasted, salted macadamia nuts (about 4 oz.)
- 4 skinless free range chicken breasts
- Salt and pepper
- About 2 tbsp. olive oil

Preheat oven to 375°. Put almond meal and coconut milk in separate wide, shallow bowls. In another bowl, place macadamia nuts. Rinse chicken and pat dry. Sprinkle all over with salt and pepper.

Put 2 tbsp. olive oil and 2 tbsp. butter in a large frying pan over medium heat. Dredge chicken in almond meal, shaking off excess; dip into coconut milk, letting excess drip off; then press into nut mixture to coat on all sides. Lay chicken in frying pan in a single layer and cook until golden brown on the bottom, 3 to 4 minutes. With a spatula, turn pieces (taking care not to break off nut coating) and brown on the other side, 2 to 3 minutes longer. Transfer chicken to a baking pan and bake until no longer pink in center of thickest part (cut to test), 15 to 20 minutes.

Miso Soup

- 4 cups cold water
- 6 – inch piece of kombu
- ¼ cup bonito flakes
- ¼ cup brown rice miso (there are so many varieties available these days).
- ¼ block tofu, cut into ½ inch cubes
- 1 scallion, thinly sliced

Place kombu and water in a saucepan and bring to a simmer, uncovered, over medium heat. Remove kombu after about 5 minutes. Stir in bonito flakes then remove from heat and let sit for 5 minutes. Strain the broth, pressing all liquids from flakes with the back of the spoon. Return broth into pan and heat slightly again. Add the tofu and scallions then simmer for about two minutes. Turn off heat and add miso to broth using a small strainer and spoon. Let your miso soup sit for a few minutes before serving.

Sometimes I add very thinly sliced young won bok, but simplicity and a flavorful stock are the keys to this traditional miso soup.

Lentil Loaf
- 1 cup green lentils
- 4 – inch piece kombu
- ½ bay leaf
- ¾ teaspoon oregano
- ½ cup bulghur
- ½ cup oatmeal (uncooked)
- ½ cup minced scallion
- 2 cloves garlic, minced
- ½ teaspoon basil
- 1 tablespoon extra virgin oil
- 1 teaspoon lemon juice
- 2 tablespoons barley miso thinned in 2 tablespoons water
- ½ cup minced parsley (optional)

Wash the lentils and combine with kombu, bay leaf, ¼ teaspoon of the oregano, and 3 cups water in large sauce pan. Bring to a boil then lower to a slow simmer and cook with lid ajar for 30 – 40 minutes or until lentils are tender and most of the liquid is absorbed. Monitor your lentils to avoid burning.

When lentils are cooked, they should be moist. If dry, add a little more water or stock. Add the oatmeal, bulghur, ½ teaspoon oregano and all remaining ingredients and mix well. Press mixture in an oiled loaf dish or pan, cover with foil, and bake at 350 degrees F. for 45 minutes or till done. Remove foil for the last 15 minutes. Cool on a wire rack for at least 30 minutes, which makes it easier to remove from pan. Serve with your favorite gravy or other sauce and garnish with a sprig of parsley. Its nice to add lightly steamed broccoli and/or braised cherry tomatoes.

Hijiki Salad

- 4 medium carrots
- 1 medium beet
- 1 medium red onion, chopped finely
- 1 ounce (oz.) hijiki seaweed, dry
- 1 teaspoon ginger finely grated or powder
- 1 oz. apple cider vinegar
- 1 oz. raw, unfiltered sesame oil
- 1 tablespoon liquid amino or tamari
- Black pepper and kelp to taste

Soak hijiki for 20 minutes, drain and chop. Clean carrots and beet well (cut off tops and ends). Grate carrots and beets and mix hijiki into it. Add ginger, oil, vinegar, liquid amino or tamari and spices. Adjust spices to taste.

Avocado/Beet Dressing

- 1 raw organic washed beet
- 1 avocado or more depending on its size
- 1 clove garlic
- 1 small thin piece of fresh ginger
- Liquid amino or tamari to taste
- Apple cider vinegar to taste (small amount)
- Flax seed oil (small amount)
- Water, just enough for the right consistency
- Squeeze of lemon (so avocado doesn't turn color)

Put in blender and blend to a creamy consistency.

Raw Creamed Strawberry Pie

Crust

- 2 cups pecans

- 4 – 6 medjool dates, pitted
- Cinnamon (pinch)

Combine pecans and dates in a blender. Divide into two equal portions and press one into pie dish. Sprinkle with cinnamon (optional). Add sliced bananas in a layer and spread the second crust on top and press into place.

Filing
- 2 – 3 ripe bananas, sliced

Topping
- ¾ cup strawberries or other berries that are in season
- 1 cup macadamia nuts or cashews
- 4 – 6 soaked dates

Mix in blender with just enough water to move the blade. Pour mixture over pie.

Chili Pepper Water
- 1 quart spring water
- 1 ½ teaspoon sea salt
- 1 - 2 cloves garlic
- 1 - 2 chili peppers

Blend well in a blender, refrigerate and use during meals. This is a great way to improve your immune system, circulation and mineral imbalances. I drink 2 – 4 ounces per day during meals. Adjust the garlic and chili peppers according to your taste.

Dashimaki Tamago
4 Eggs, 1/4 cups stock (dashi),
Mixture: (1/2 table spoons soy, salt, 1/2 tablespoons mirin),
Oil

Directions

- Put 1/4 cups of stock into a bowl add the mixture soy-salt-mirin mixture and stir.
- Beat 4 eggs in another bowl then add to above.
- Thinly coat a square frying pan with oil. Wipe out the surplus oil with a cloth or paper towel. Pour 1/3 of the mixture into the frying pan, and spread it evenly by jiggling the pan.
- After the surface of (3) hardens slightly, roll it up to one end of the frying pan.
- Move the rolled egg to the opposite side and oil the bottom surface. Add another 1/3 of (2) into the pan, and roll it up after the surface of (3) comes has hardened.
- Repeat (5) with the last 1/3 of the mixture.
- Pick (6) up and let it cool and cut.

Index

Hawaiian Definitions

Aho'ole – Breathless State.

Akua – God, goddess, spirit, divine.

Ala – Awaken.

Alo – In the presence of, the connection we have to all things including Kumukahi.

'Aumakua – Family or personal god(s), deified ancestor who might assume the shape of an animal, describes frequency that exists in all things.

Ipu Kea – Lit. White gourd, term used in Kona, Hawaii during my grandfather's days to mean Caucasian, white foreigner.

Hā – The essence of life from where the evolutionary process unfolds. Breath of life.

Ha Ho'opapau - Breath concentration, focus breathing.

Ha Maka'ala - Breathing awareness or conscious breathing.

Hana – Work, function.

Hanu i loko – Inhale

Hanu i waho – Exhale

Ha'ole – Without breath.

Ha Pule - Prayer ritual using the essence of Ha.

Hiamoe – Sleep.

Hokule'a – A double hull canoe from Hawaii; Star of joy/happiness, Arcturus. Also a term used to describe the "minds eye."

Ho'ohana hou – Recyle, reuse.

Ho'okuano'o – Meditation.

Ho'o lomi – The ability to communicate to the core of the bones with your hands.

Ho'o lokahi - Harmonize

Ho'o maika'i – gratitude, grateful.

Ho'o mana'o – will power, desire.

Ho'o manawanui – To have patience.

Ho'o pono – A concept of bringing balance into one's life, the action of forgiveness, severing unwanted energetic cords.

Hūnā – To hide, conceal, disguise.

Huna – Hidden secret, particle, as in an atom.

'Ike – To see, know, feel, knowledge with wisdom, comprehension.

'Ike Kino – Mind body, an intelligence with the body, DNA strands.

Kahuna – Priest, sorcerer, minister, magician, wizard, expert in any profession. In the 1800's the DeFacto Government established laws that gave modern doctors, surgeons, and dentists the title of *Kahuna*.

Kalo - Taro

Kanaka Anela – Angelic humans, people who have compassion and empathy.

Kaulike – Equality, balance, alike.

Kanaka – Humans, people.

Kanaka Maoli – Full blooded Hawaiian, host culture, or original inhabitants.

Kaona - Hidden meaning, as in Hawaiian poetry; concealed reference, as to a person, place, or thing; words with double meanings.

Kapu – Sacred, holy, forbidden, ancient Hawaiian laws.

Kino Lau – Many bodies, many forms.

Ku'auhau - Genealogy, pedigree, lineage, old traditions.

Kuamo'o – Pathway or purpose of life chant.

Kuapo – Replace, exchange.

Kukakuka – Discussion, consult, talk story.

Kuleana – Responsibility, title, piece of land.

Kumu – Foundation, tree trunk, teacher, source, beginning.

kumu a'o ku'auhau – Lineage of teachers.

Kumukahi – One/Original Source.

Kumu 'Ike – Source intelligence.

Kumu Ola – Source of health, part of Kumukahi.

Kupuna – Grandparent, elder, ancestor, starting point, source; growing.

La'au – Tree, plant, strength, medicine.

La'au Lapa'au – Lit. Curing, medicine.

Lauhala – Pandanus odoratissimus tree.

Lokahi – Unity, harmony, embracing diversity.

Loli'ana – To change, influence, transmute.

Lomilomi – Hawaiian bodywork therapy, describes energy in motion.

Mahalo – Thank you.

Ma'i – Ill, disease, sickness.

Makahiki – Year, age, annual; Ancient festival beginning about the middle of October and lasting about four months, with sports and religious festivities and kapu on war.

Make 'Ole – Without death, deathless.

Maluhia – Peace, tranquility, quiet.

Mamao aku ola – Distant healing.

Mana – Life force, strong spirit, spiritual energy.

Mana Lomi – A form of lomi that focuses on problem solving.

Mana'o – Thought, opinion, meaning, desire.

Mana'o Ma'i – Thinking disease.

Mana'o Pa'a – Determination.

Mana'o Pono – Will power.

Na'ana'au – Small intestines.

Na'au – Intestines, gut feelings, intuition.

Na'au Pono – Trust, knowing, intuition.

Na Koa – Warriors

Ni'ihau – A privately own island north of Kauai whose inhabitants are pure Hawaiians.

Na'auao – Wisdom, enlightened, knowledge, intelligent.

Na'auao 'ike mua - foresight, visionary.

Na'auao ola Hawaii - Hawaiian wisdom of health.

No'ono'o – Thought, concentrate, reflection, meditation, to consider.

No'ono'o pono - think carefully, positive thinking, thoughtful, self-discipline.

'Ohana – Family, relative, related, lineage.

'Oki – To cut; sever, as in severing unwanted energetic cords.

'Okina – a glottal stop (')

Ola – Life, health.

'Onipa'a – Fixed, resolute, determined.

'Opu – Stomach.

Piko – Umbilical connection, center, node, chakra points.

Piko Pu'uwai – Heart chakra.

Po'e Kanaka - Human

Pono – Alignment, in perfect order, excellence, balance, homeostasis.

Pono 'Ole – Imbalance, without alignment.

Pueo – Hawaiian owl.

Pule - Prayer

Puna – Spring (of water).

Puna Ola – Spring of Life, endless health.

Uha – Colon, large intestines.

Waihona 'Ike – Mind intelligence.

---

[i] (For calculations detail, see "Unnecessary Hospitalization." Sources: HCUPnet, Healthcare Cost and Utilization Project, Agency for Healthcare Research and Quality, Rockville, MD. Available at: http://www.ahrq.gov/data/hcup/hcupnet. htm. Accessed December 18, 2003. Siu AL, Sonnenberg FA, Manning WG, et al. Inappropriate use of hospitals in a randomized trial of health insurance plans. N Engl J Med. 1986 Nov 13; 315(20): 1259-66. Siu AL, Manning WG, Benjamin B. Patient, provider and hospital characteristics associated with inappropriate hospitalization. Am J Public Health. 1990 Oct; 80(10): 1253-6. Eriksen BO, Kristiansen IS, Nord E, et al. The cost of inappropriate admissions: a study of health benefits and resource utilization in a department of internal medicine. J Intern Med. 1999 Oct; 246(4): 379-87)